BIBLE DOCTRINE

FOUNDATIONS OF FAITH

BIBLE DOCTRINE

FOUNDATIONS OF FAITH

BIBLE DOCTRINE

Copyright - © 2023

First Edition: 11/23

ISBN: 9798866080472

Printed in the United States of America

All rights reserved. No part of this book may be reproduced in any form without permission from the author, except as permitted by U.S. copyright law.

BIBLE DOCTRINE is a compilation of studies and personal revelations I have received, through Bible College, listening to other anointed preachers and teachers, and from some amazing books I have on my shelf.

Isaiah 58 Ministries

25837 S. 4420 Rd,

Vinita, OK 74301 USA

To request permission, contact Mark Visser

mark_visser@me.com

https://isaiah58church.org

FOUNDATIONS OF FAITH

BIBLE DOCTRINE

FOUNDATIONS OF FAITH

BIBLE DOCTRINE

BIBLE DOCTRINE is what we stand on in our faith and it is what the church is built on.

We are empowered by The Holy Spirit to equip saints for ministry and win souls for the Kingdom of God.

We are building prophetic wells where you will be encouraged, equipped, endorsed and empowered by The Holy Spirit to bring your community to Jesus.

We provide apostolic / prophetic oversight to those who want to join us in building prophetic wells in person or online.

We train and equip in the prophetic, through teaching, imparting and delivering the now word of God.

Isaiah 58 Ministries
25837 S. 4420 Rd., Vinita, OK 74016

Visit with us for Sunday morning worship, 10:30 AM

FOUNDATIONS OF FAITH

BIBLE DOCTRINE

FOUNDATIONS OF FAITH

DEDICATION

To my amazing magnificent wife, best friend and cherished love of my life; the wonderful mother of our children and best granny ever; my sister in Christ, my Ezer-Kanegdo, helper and friend, who always encourages, inspires and lifts me up. I love you, and bless you, Caron Visser.

You are truly the Proverbs 31:30 woman, "A woman who fears the Lord will be greatly praised."

Thank you for motivating me and encouraging me to put pen to paper and write.

BIBLE DOCTRINE

FOUNDATIONS OF FAITH

BIBLE DOCTRINES

DOCTRINE AND CREED 10
DOCTRINE OF GOD..26
DOCTRINE OF JESUS CHRIST 48
DOCTRINE OF THE HOLY SPIRIT 116
DOCTRINE OF THE BIBLE..160
DOCTRINE OF MAN..236
DOCTRINE OF FAITH...248
DOCTRINE OF ANGELS..268
DOCTRINE OF THE TWO KINGDOMS..331
DOCTRINE OF ESCHATOLOGY 335
BIBLIOGRAPHY..351

FOUNDATIONS OF FAITH

BIBLE DOCTRINE

DOCTRINE AND CREED

The English term "doctrine" finds its origins in the Latin word "doctrina" and can be succinctly defined as "teaching or instruction." When it comes to Christian doctrine, we delve into the core beliefs of Christians. This extends to a comprehensive exploration of what the entire Bible conveys on a particular subject, encompassing the "doctrine" of Christ, the "doctrine" of God, and the "doctrine" of the church. These doctrines encapsulate what Christians believe about these subjects, derived from the teachings within the Bible.

While the terms "doctrine" and "theology" are sometimes used interchangeably, they hold subtle distinctions. The broader term, theology or Christian theology, pertains to the study of the God presented in the Bible. On the other hand, Doctrine delves into specific teachings like theological inquiries, like the "doctrine" of salvation or the "doctrine" of death.

While not explicitly featuring the term "theology," the New Testament offers a trove of references to Christian doctrine, with over forty such mentions. Christian doctrine encompasses the teachings of Jesus Christ as conveyed in the four gospels, alongside the teachings about Jesus Christ found throughout the remainder of the New Testament.

BIBLE DOCTRINE

Doctrine is most crucial to the foundation of faith.

Acts 16:30-31 Without true doctrine you cannot be saved.

2 John 9 Whoever abides in the doctrine of CHRIST has both the FATHER and the SON.

Hebrews 13:9 Do not be led away by diverse and strange teachings, for it is good for the heart to be strengthened by grace, not by foods, which have not benefited those devoted to them.

1 Timothy 6:3-4 If anyone teaches a different doctrine and does not agree with the sound words of our Lord Jesus Christ and the teaching that accords with godliness, he is puffed up with conceit and understands nothing.

Our understanding and revelation of GOD define our doctrine and theology of GOD, though in no ways can our doctrine or theology of GOD change who GOD is.

The doctrine and theology of the church are what define the parameters of faith in Christ.

True doctrine divides light from darkness, right from wrong, and life from death.

BIBLE DOCTRINE

True doctrine will save you from false theology. 2 Timothy. 4:1-4 I solemnly charge you before God and Christ Jesus, who is going to judge the living and the dead, and because of His appearing and His kingdom: Proclaim the message; persist in it whether convenient or not; rebuke, correct, and encourage with great patience and teaching. For the time will come when they will not tolerate sound doctrine, but according to their own desires, will multiply teachers for themselves because they have an itch to hear something new. They will turn away from hearing the truth and will turn aside to myths.

True doctrine well established you. Ephesians 4:14 Then we will no longer be little children, tossed by the waves and blown around by every wind of teaching, by human cunning with cleverness in the techniques of deceit.

True doctrine will help you edify GOD. 2 Timothy 2:15 Be diligent to present yourself approved to God, a worker who doesn't need to be ashamed, correctly teaching the word of truth.

True doctrine will help you to equip yourself. Ephesians 6:10-17 Finally, be strengthened by the Lord and by His vast strength. Put on the full armor of God so that you can stand against the tactics of the Devil. For our battle is not against flesh and blood, but against the rulers, against the authorities, against the world powers of this darkness, against the spiritual forces of evil in the heavens. This is why you must take up the full armor of God, so that you may be able to resist in the evil day, and having prepared everything, to take your stand. Stand, therefore, with truth like a belt around your waist, righteousness like armor on your chest, and your feet sandaled with readiness for the gospel of peace. In every situation take the shield of faith, and with it you will be able to extinguish all the flaming arrows of the evil one. Take the helmet of salvation, and the sword of the Spirit, which is God's word.

No word has been so successfully twisted by the devil today as the word doctrine.

Your doctrine is the fundamentals of your Creed and this makes up your theology.

Your doctrine and creeds are the theologies you live by and the essentials of your faith.

Your creed is the immutable teachings of God, taught through His Word, the Bible.

The devil will always try and twist your creed and bring in false doctrines and theologies.

It is most important to know the Truth for it is only The Truth that will set us free.

BIBLE DOCTRINE

Jesus says that some are teaching as doctrines the commandments of men. Matthew 15:9 For from the heart come evil thoughts, murders, adulteries, sexual immoralities, thefts, false testimonies, blasphemies.

Paul says we must to watch out for those who cause divisions and create obstacles contrary to the doctrine that you have been taught; avoid them. Romans 16:17 Now I urge you, brothers, to watch out for those who cause dissensions and obstacles contrary to the doctrine you have learned. Avoid them,

Paul commanded Timothy to teach any different doctrine. 1 Tim. 1:3,4 As I urged you when I went to Macedonia, remain in Ephesus so that you may instruct certain people not to teach different doctrine or to pay attention to myths and endless genealogies.

There are four viewpoints on theology.
Biblical Theology is the viewpoint from the biblical writers and recognized teachers of Scripture, while historical theology is the viewpoint undertaken within the practices of history and culture. Then, systematic theology is the viewpoint that arranges biblical truths and theological voices of history in consistent teachings and practical theology is the viewpoint from an academic discipline to critically discern the truths of the Christian faith.

BIBLE DOCTRINE

The best way to ensure you are not deceived by hearing a false doctrine or theology is to know your Creed and your Doctrine, so well that you can discern error right away.

BIBLE DOCTRINE

CREED OF THE CHURCH

The Creeds of the Church have been the primary centerpiece of Christian apologetics and Christian faith. Its truths remind us of the essence of our faith and that it is most important to contend for the faith that was once and for all delivered to the saints.

Jude 3 Dear friends, although I was eager to write you about the salvation we share, I found it necessary to write and exhort you to contend for the faith that was delivered to the saints once and for all.

The Creeds are summaries of the doctrine that we Christians believe to be taught in the Bible. Creeds provide a theological mirror of the Bible's fundamental doctrine. The word "creed" comes to us from the Latin "Credo" or "I believe". Creeds are essentially summaries of the teachings of scripture, never formulated to invent fundamental doctrines. Creeds were developed to address particular heresies and to defend the authenticity of Scripture.

The 4th century Nicene Creed, for instance, was formulated expressly to combat a Christological heresy called Arianism, which denied the deity of Christ and taught that He was a created being (Jehovah's Witnesses belief have revived this heresy).

As you explore the creeds of the Church, we pray that God would make Hebrew 10:23 true and alive to you. "Let us hold on to the confession of our hope without wavering, for He who promised is faithful.:

BIBLE DOCTRINE

Creed Of Irenaeus, Bishop Of Lyons – Ad.180

The Church believes in one God, the Father Almighty, Maker of heaven, and earth, and the sea, and all things that are in them; and in one Christ Jesus, the Son of God, who became incarnate for our salvation; and in the Holy Spirit, who proclaimed through the prophets the dispensations of God, and the advents, and the birth from a virgin, and the passion, and the resurrection from the dead, and the ascension into heaven in the flesh of the beloved Christ Jesus, our Lord, and his manifestation from heaven in the glory of the Father to gather all things in one, and to raise up anew all flesh of the whole human race, in order that to Christ Jesus, our Lord, and God, and Savior, and King, according to the will of the invisible Father, every knee should bow, of things in heaven, and things in earth, and things under the earth, and that every tongue should confess to him, and that he should execute just judgment towards all; that he may send spiritual wickedness, and the angels who transgressed and became apostates, together with the ungodly and unrighteous and wicked and profane among men, into everlasting fire; but may, in the exercise of his grace, confer immortality on the righteous, and holy, and those who have kept his commandments, and have persevered in his love, some from the beginning, and others from their repentance, and may surround them with everlasting glory.

Sanctifier of the faith of those who believe in the Father and the Son and the Holy Ghost.

BIBLE DOCTRINE

We believe that there is one God, and no other besides the Maker of the world, who produced the universe out of nothing, by his word sent forth first of all; that his Logos, called his Son, was seen in the name of God in various ways by the patriarchs, was always heard in the prophets, at last was sent down, from the Spirit and the power of God the Father, into the Virgin Mary, was made flesh in her womb, and born of her, appeared as Jesus Christ; then he preached the Law and the new promise of the kingdom of heaven; wrought miracles; was nailed to the cross; rose again on the third day; was caught up to the heavens; and sat down at the right hand of the Father; sent in his place the power of the Holy Spirit; to guide the believers; he will come again with glory to take the saints into the glory of eternal life and the celestial promises, and to judge the wicked with eternal fire, after the resuscitation of both; with restitution of the flesh.

The Creed Of Jerusalem – A.D. 314

We believe in one GOD the Father of all - Sovereign maker of Heaven and earth, and all things visible and invisible, and in one Lord Jesus Christ the only begotten Son of GOD. Begotten of the Father before all ages - Light of light – True GOD of True GOD - Begotten not made - Of one substance with the Father through Him all things were made - Who for us men and for our salvation came down from the heavens and was made flesh of the Holy Spirit; the Virgin Mary and became man and was crucified for us under Pontius pilot - Suffered and was buried and rose again on the third day according to the Scriptures - Ascended into the heavens and sitteth at the right hand of the Father, and cometh again with glory to judge the living and the dead, of whose kingdom there will be no end, And in the Holy Spirit the Lord and the life giver that proceedeth from the Father who with the father and son is worshiped together and glorified together who spoke through the prophets in one holy Catholic and apostolic church, We acknowledge one baptism unto remission of sins we look forward for the resurrection of the dead and the life of the age to come

BIBLE DOCTRINE

The Nicene Creed - Ad.325

I believe in one God, the Father Almighty, Maker of heaven and earth, and of all things visible and invisible.

And in one Lord Jesus Christ, the only-begotten Son of God, begotten of the Father before all worlds; God of God, Light of Light, very God of very God; begotten, not made, being of one substance with the Father, by whom all things were made.

Who, for us men for our salvation, came down from heaven, and was incarnate by the Holy Spirit of the virgin Mary, and was made man; and was crucified also for us under Pontius Pilate; He suffered and was buried; and the third day He rose again, according to the Scriptures; and ascended into heaven, and sits on the right hand of the Father; and He shall come again, with glory, to judge the quick and the dead; whose kingdom shall have no end.

And I believe in the Holy Ghost, the Lord and Giver of Life; who proceeds from the Father [and the Son]; who with the Father and the Son together is worshipped and glorified; who spoke by the prophets.

And I believe one holy catholic and apostolic Church. I acknowledge one baptism for the remission of sins; and I look for the resurrection of the dead, and the life of the world to come. Amen.

BIBLE DOCTRINE

The Creed

(This Creed has been adapted from the above creeds.)

GOD

We believe in One GOD our Father, all Sovereign maker of heaven and maker of earth, maker of things visible and invisible.

GOD is all-powerful, all-knowing, and all-loving.

We believe this world and all humanity began with GOD and is all held together by GOD.

We believe GOD is eternally existent in three persons:

GOD is the Father. GOD is the Son. GOD is the Holy Spirit.

We believe GOD is three in one and is co-equal known as The Trinity.

JESUS CHRIST

We believe in Jesus Christ. We believe Jesus is 100% the son of man as Jesus, and Christ is 100% the Son of GOD as Christ.

We believe Christ is God the Son, the second person of the Trinity.

We believe that Christ is The Word of God, begotten of the Father before all ages, light of light, true God of true God, begotten not made, of one substance with the Father, through whom all things were made.

Who for us human beings and for our salvation Christ came down from the heavens and was made flesh by the power of the Holy Spirit and born as Jesus, to God as His Father and the virgin Mary as His earthly mother.

Jesus is the only man ever to have lived a sinless life.

Jesus Christ was despised by his own people, was crucified for us under Pontius Pilate, died and was buried, and rose again on the third day, ascended into the heavens to sit on the right hand of the Father.

Jesus died on the cross for humankind and thus atoned for our sins through the shedding of His blood.

Jesus rose from the dead on the third day, ascended to the right hand of the Father, and will return again in power and glory.

Jesus Christ is the only way to the Father and He alone offers remission of sins and resurrection of the flesh and life everlasting.

HOLY SPIRIT

We believe in the Holy Spirit, life giver, which proceeds from the Father, who with the Father and Son is worshipped together and glorified together.

We believe that the Holy Spirit was given at Pentecost and is the promise of the Father, sent by Jesus after His ascension.

We believe the Holy Spirit is our counselor, comforter and friend who has given to us His fruit and His gifts to show the Glory of GOD to us, for us and through us to the rest of the world for the purpose of bringing Glory to GOD.

BIBLE DOCTRINE

We believe in baptism into the Holy Spirit that gives to us the power of GOD to demonstrate the goodness, grace, power and salvation of GOD to us, though us and to be witnesses of Jesus Christ to the whole earth.

BIBLE

We believe that the Holy Bible is the inspired Word of God.

The Word of God is alive and active in bringing healing and restoration between God and mankind.

The Word of God will never contradict itself whether in written form as in the Holy Bible or in spoken form, past, present or in the future.

The Word of God is accurate, authoritative and applicable to our everyday lives.

CHURCH

We believe that Jesus Christ is the Head of the body of Christ, the Church, the Ekklesia, the communion of the Saints, which is made up of people from every tongue, tribe and nation that live in the Truth of the Word of God, and believe in Him alone.

For there is one Lord, one Faith and one Baptism and that is into Jesus Christ.

RETURN OF CHRIST

BIBLE DOCTRINE

We believe that Jesus Christ will return in glory to judge the living and the dead.

We believe that a home has been prepared for both those alive in Christ and those dead to Christ for the people of the past, the present and those still to come.

REPENTANCE and SALVATION

We believe repentance is the commitment to turn away from sin in every area of our lives and to follow Christ and seek His Kingdom first. We believe in order to receive salvation, we must repent from our sins.

We believe only Jesus Christ can forgive sin and full submission Jesus Christ as Lord of your life is the most crucial aspect of your relationship with God.

We believe we are saved by grace through faith in Jesus Christ as our Lord and Savior.

We believe salvation is a gift from God, not a result of our good works or of any human effort.

We believe that every individual whose faith is in Christ Jesus should have one common vision acted out in various ways.

The vision of the Great Commission.

KINGDOM OF GOD

We believe in the Kingdom of GOD with power, signs, wonders, works of miracles, healing, restoration, deliverance and salvation from sin.

We believe in the equipping of the saints and building up of the Body of Christ until we all reach unity in the faith and in the knowledge of the Son (Word) of God becoming mature as one body of the fullness of Christ.

ETERNITY

We believe people were created for eternity.

We believe we will either exist eternally separated from GOD by sin or will exist eternally with God through forgiveness and salvation.

We believe that Heaven is the eternal dwelling place for all believers through the Gospel of Jesus Christ.

We believe the unbelievers will be judged by God, separated from GOD where they will be eternally tormented with the Devil and the Fallen Angels.

We believe that our Statement of Faith is the very truth of God the Father, and not the invention of any man.

BIBLE DOCTRINE

DOCTRINE OF GOD

Isaiah 45:5-6, "I am the Lord, and there is no other, apart from me there is no other. I will strengthen you though you have not acknowledged me. So that from the rising of the sun to the place of its setting, men may know there is none besides me. I am the Lord and there is no other."

The Bible does not attempt to prove that God exists. Rather, it invites us to look around us, within us, and into the vast cosmos above, and there, in the intricate tapestry of existence, we find the undeniable affidavit of His existence.

Every creature in the universe, from the smallest ant to the mightiest whale, from the humblest daisy to the grandest redwood tree, is a testament to God's creativity. The universe itself, with its countless constellations, galaxies, stars, and planets, testify to His boundless creativity. We are not isolated beings in a random world; we are part of a grand design to singularly be the image bearer of God.

The God of the Bible is the only true God, who stands alone, set apart from all other gods, deities, and idols that humanity has crafted throughout history. He is a jealous holy God, not in a petty or selfish sense, who protect His deity with a vengeance of any who try to rise up above Him.

He desires His children to live abundantly, unburdened by confusion, rebellion, and unbelief that false gods may bring into their lives.

God is independent, self-sufficient, and self-existent. He does not rely on us or any of His creation to validate His existence. He is the source of all existence. He is infinite and eternal, never created, and never coming into being. He is the great I AM, the supreme Creator from whom all things have sprung. While the world and its inhabitants change, our God remains constant. His character does not waver, and His purposes are eternally fixed.

The promises God makes, He keeps. His word is a rock of stability in an ever-shifting world. Hebrews 13:8 assures us of this: "Jesus Christ is the same yesterday, today, and forever."

God's presence knows no bounds. He is all-present, as described in Psalm 139:4-10. "Where can I go from your Spirit? Where can I flee from your presence?" He is everywhere, in the highest heavens and the deepest depths. His guiding hand is always with us, providing unwavering support.

God is all-knowing, as revealed in Psalm 139:2-4 You know when I sit down and when I stand up; You understand my thoughts from far away. You observe my travels and my rest; You are aware of all my ways. Before a word is on my tongue, You know all about it, LORD.

He comprehends our thoughts before they become words. He is familiar with all our ways, even before we take action.

His omnipotence is beyond question. Jeremiah 32:17 proclaims, "Ah, Sovereign Lord, you have made the heavens and the earth by your great power and outstretched arm. Nothing is hard for you." There is nothing that God cannot accomplish, no challenge too great for His might.

Philippians 4:13 reaffirms this: "I can do all things through Christ who gives me strength." and in Deuteronomy 31:6 He promises, "Be strong and courageous, do not be afraid or terrified because of them, for the Lord your God goes with you; he will never leave you nor forsake you." Our God is the omnipotent companion in our journey through life.

Our understanding of God must align with the reality of who He says He is. The Bible introduces us to Jehovah as the great "I AM who I AM," as declared in Exodus 3:14. He is an infinite, eternal, and unchangeable being, a fountain of wisdom, power, holiness, justice, goodness, and truth. God is a spirit, not confined by physical form or driven by passions. His immutable and righteous will guides His actions, all for His glory.

God is characterized by boundless love, grace, and mercy. He offers forgiveness to those who earnestly seek Him. But, He is also just and stern in His judgments, abhorring sin and holding the unrepentant accountable. Even fallen angels face eternal judgment.

In summary, our understanding of the doctrine of God shapes our relationship with Him, impacting our love, devotion, and service. He is the supreme, all-encompassing being, and knowing and living by His doctrine is essential for an authentic, fulfilling spiritual journey.

This is only the beginning of who God is, for His depth and majesty are beyond human comprehension.

In seeking to understand Matthew 6:33 we embark on a journey of discovery that leads to a more profound understanding of our Creator, our Savior, and our ever-present, unchanging God. "But seek first the kingdom of God and His righteousness, and all these things will be provided for you."

BIBLE DOCTRINE

The Names And Titles Of God.

To understand Bible Doctrine, it is most important to first understand the Names of God, as each name of God gives us insight into the attributes of God and His relationship with His people. Each name of God reveals a different aspect of His character and personality, and as we draw near and come to know the various names of God, we will gain a deeper understanding of who He is and how He is changing us daily into His perfect image and likeness.

ADONAI - Adonai is the Divine name of God, translated as Lord, master, and owner, signifying His Sovereignty of all. Colossians 1:16 For in him all things were created: things in heaven and on earth, visible and invisible, whether thrones or powers or rulers or authorities; all things have been created through him and for him.

ADONAI YISHMA - The Lord Who Hears you from the place of your desolation.
Isaiah 30:19 For you people will live on Zion in Jerusalem and will never cry again. He will show favor to you at the sound of your cry; when He hears, He will answer you.

ADONAI HOSHIA - The Lord of our Victory. Deuteronomy 20:3,4 Today you are about to engage in battle with your enemies. Do not be cowardly. Do not be afraid, alarmed, or terrified because of them. For the LORD your God is the One who goes with you to fight for you against your enemies to give you victory.

ARYEH MISHEVET Y'HUDAH - Lion of Judah. Hosea 5:14 For I am like a lion to Ephraim and like a young lion to the house of Judah. Yes, I will tear them to pieces and depart. I will carry them off, and no one can rescue them.

BA'AL – Husband. Isaiah 54:5 Indeed, your husband is your Maker — His name is Yahweh of Hosts — and the Holy One of Israel is your Redeemer; He is called the God of all the earth.

EHYEH ASHER EHYEH - I AM THAT I AM. Exodus 3:14 God replied to Moses, "I AM WHO I AM. This is what you are to say to the Israelites: I AM has sent me to you."

ELOHIM - God is the majestic ruler over all. Elohim is a plural word and the first name of GOD that sets God high above every other god. Genesis 1:1 In the beginning God created the heavens and the earth.

ELYON - The Most High GOD. Genesis 14:18 Then Melchizedek, king of Salem, brought out bread and wine; he was a priest to God Most High.

BIBLE DOCTRINE

EL ROI - The God Who Sees Me. Genesis 16:13 So she called the LORD who spoke to her: The God Who Sees, for she said, "In this place, have I actually seen the One who sees me?"

EL SHADDAI - Lord God Almighty. Genesis 17:1 I AM GOD Almighty. Live in My presence and be blameless.

EL OLAM - The everlasting God. Genesis 21:33 Abraham planted a tamarisk tree in Beer-sheba, and there he called on the name of Yahweh, the Everlasting God.

EL QANNA - The jealous, zealous God. Exodus 34:14 You are never to bow down to another god because Yahweh, being jealous by nature, is a jealous God.

EL HAI - -The Living God. Deuteronomy 5:26 For who out of all mankind has heard the voice of the living God speaking from the fire, as we have, and lived?

EL OHIM EMET - True God. Jeremiah 10:10 Yahweh is the true God; He is the living God and eternal King.

EL NOSEY - Forgiving God.

BIBLE DOCTRINE

Micah 7:18 Who is a God like You, removing iniquity and passing over rebellion for the remnant of His inheritance? He does not hold on to His anger forever, because He delights in faithful love.

EL HESED - God of Kindness. Psalms 86:4-7 ...For You, Lord, are kind and ready to forgive, rich in faithful love to all who call on You.

ELOHEY YISH'I - God of My Salvation. Micah 7:7 But I will look to the LORD; I will wait for the God of my salvation. My God will hear me.

ELOHIM HECHAKHAM - The Wise God. Romans 16:27 to the only wise God, through Jesus Christ — to Him be the glory forever! Amen.

EL SIMCHATI - My Joy. Psalms 16:11 You reveal the path of life to me; in Your presence is abundant joy; in Your right hand are eternal pleasures.

EZRATI - My Helper. Exodus 18:4 The God of my father was my helper and delivered me from Pharaoh's sword.

GO'ALI - My Redeemer. Isaiah 44:6 This is what the LORD, the King of Israel and its Redeemer, the LORD of Hosts, says: I am the first and I am the last. There is no God but Me.

HA'OLAM - Light of the World.

FOUNDATIONS OF FAITH

Psalms 18:28 The heavens were made by the word of the LORD, and all the stars, by the breath of His mouth.

ISH MILCHAMAH - Warrior. Exodus 15:3 The LORD is a warrior; Yahweh is His name.

JEHOVAH JIREH - The Lord will Provide. Genesis 22:14 The LORD Will Provide,

JEHOVAH NISSI - -The Lord My Banner Exodus 17:15 The Lord Is My Banner.

JEHOVAH SHALOM - The Lord my Peace. Judges 6:24 So Gideon built an altar to the LORD there and called it Yahweh Shalom.

JEHOVAH SABAOTH - The Lord of Hosts. 1 Samuel 1:3 This man would go up from his town every year to worship and to sacrifice to the LORD of Hosts at Shiloh,...

JEHOVAH MEKODDESH - The Lord my sanctifier. Exodus 31:13 Tell the Israelites: You must observe My Sabbaths, for it is a sign between Me and you throughout your generations so that you will know that I am Yahweh who sets you apart.

JEHOVAH RAAH - The Lord is My Shepherd. Psalms 23:1 The LORD is my shepherd; there is nothing I lack.

JEHOVAH TSIDKENU - The Lord my Righteousness. Jeremiah 23:6 In His days Judah will be saved, and Israel will dwell securely. This is what He will be named: Yahweh Our Righteousness.

JEHOVAH SHAMMAH - The Lord is there. Ezekiel 48:35 The perimeter of the city will be six miles, and the name of the city from that day on will be: Yahweh Is There."

JEHOVAH RAPHA - The Lord my Healer.
Exodus 15:26 He said, "If you will carefully obey the LORD your God, do what is right in His eyes, pay attention to His commands, and keep all His statutes, I will not inflict any illnesses on you that I inflicted on the Egyptians. For I am Yahweh who heals you."

JEHOVAH SABOATH - The Lord Creator. 1 Samuel 1:3 This man would go up from his town every year to worship and to sacrifice to the LORD of Hosts at Shiloh...

JEHOVAH MASHACH - The Lord my Anointer. Isaiah 61:1 The Spirit of the Lord GOD is on Me, because the LORD has anointed Me

JEHOVAH UZZI - The Lord My Powerful Strength. Psalms 28:7 The LORD is my strength and my shield; my heart trusts in Him, and I am helped.

JEHOVAH MAGENESIS - The Lord My Shield. Genesis 15:1 Do not be afraid, Abram. I am your shield; your reward will be very great.

JEHOVAH HOSEENU - The Lord My Maker. Psalms 95:6 Come, let us worship and bow down; let us kneel before the LORD our Maker.

JEHOVAH EL-HANUN - The Lord of Compassion.
Exodus 34:6 Then the LORD passed in front of him and proclaimed: Yahweh — Yahweh is a compassionate and gracious God, slow to anger and rich in faithful love and truth,

JEHOVAH RUACH - The Spirit of the Lord. 1 Samuel 16:13 ...and the Spirit of the LORD took control of David from that day forward.

MAYIM HAYIM - Living Water. Jeremiah 2:13 For My people have committed a double evil: They have abandoned Me, the fountain of living water, ...

MELEKH HAGOYIM - King of the Nations. Jeremiah 10:6,7 Yahweh, there is no one like You. You are great; Your name is great in power. Who should not fear You, King of the nations? it is what You deserve. For among all the wise people of the nations and among all their kingdoms, there is no one like You.

BIBLE DOCTRINE

NISHMAT CHAYIM - Breath of Life. Psalms 33:6 The heavens were made by the word of the LORD, and all the stars, by the breath of His mouth.

OHEV - Friend. Exodus 33:11 The LORD spoke with Moses face to face, just as a man speaks with his friend. Then Moses would return to the camp, but his assistant, the young man Joshua son of Nun, would not leave the inside of the tent.

RUACH HECHAZON - Spirit of Revelation. 1 Samuel 9:15 ...the LORD had informed Samuel,

TOV ADONAI - The Lord is Good. Psalms 25:8 The LORD is good and upright;

TIKVATI - My Hope. Psalms 52:9 I will put my hope in Your Name, for it is good.

TZVAOT – Captain of the Army 1 Samuel 17:45 I come against you in the name of Yahweh of Hosts, the God of Israel's armies — you have defied Him.

ZIMRATI - My Song. Exodus 15:2 The LORD is my strength and my song; He has become my salvation. This is my God, and I will praise Him, my father's God, and I will exalt Him.

FOUNDATIONS OF FAITH

BIBLE DOCTRINE

God Revealed

God is diverse, yet singular in the identity of being triune as the Three in One, yet personal as the One in Three. God is most profound and all-encompassing. God creates and destroys, provides, and promotes. God cares, hears, hates. grieves, and loves. God's essence is a complex, harmonious blend that transcends simple understanding and confuses the wise, inviting intimacy into the intricate tapestry of His Divine attributes.

God is self-existent, eternal, and Sovereign, infinitely present, all-powerful, and all-knowing. God is light, God is goodness and God is love; righteous, just, and merciful. God is immutable and inscrutable, God is distinct from creation, as God created all things. God dwells within the universe and above the highest stars in the universe. God is all wise, faithful, and always near to those who seek Him. The incomprehensible and eternal nature of God defines a reality both beyond reason and understanding, yet in His goodness and kindness He has created us in His express Image and likeness and given to us the Mind of Christ.

GOD is Spirit. John 4:24 God is spirit, and those who worship Him must worship in spirit and truth.

GOD creates. Genesis 1:1 In the beginning God created the heavens and the earth.

GOD destroys. Genesis 18:21 I will go down to see if what they have done justifies the cry that has come up to Me. If not, I will find out.

GOD provides. Psalms 104:27 All of them wait for You.

GOD promotes. Psalms 75:7 for God is the Judge: He brings down one and exalts another.

GOD cares. 1 Peter 5:7 casting all your care on Him, because He cares about you.

GOD hears and sees. Psalms 94:9 Can the One who shaped the ear not hear, the One who formed the eye not see?

GOD hates. Proverbs 6:16 The LORD hates six things; in fact, seven are detestable to Him

GOD grieves. Genesis 6:6 The LORD regretted that He had made man on the earth, and He was grieved in His heart.

GOD loves. John 3:16 For God loved the world in this way: He gave His One and Only Son, so that everyone who believes in Him will not perish but have eternal life.

BIBLE DOCTRINE

GOD is one. Deuteronomy 6:4,5 Listen, Israel: The LORD our God, the LORD is One.

GOD is a trinity. Matthew 28:19 Go, therefore, and make disciples of all nations, baptizing them in the name of the Father and of the Son and of the Holy Spirit,

GOD is self-existent. Exodus 3:13,14 Then Moses asked God, "If I go to the Israelites and say to them: The God of your fathers has sent me to you, and they ask me, 'What is His name?' what should I tell them?" God replied to Moses, "I AM WHO I AM. This is what you are to say to the Israelites: I AM has sent me to you."

GOD is eternal. Deuteronomy 33:27 The God of old is your dwelling place, and underneath are the everlasting arms. He drives out the enemy before you and commands, "Destroy!"

GOD is sovereign. Psalms 135:6 Yahweh does whatever He pleases in heaven and on earth, in the seas and all the depths.

GOD is light. 1 John 1:5 God is light, and there is absolutely no darkness in Him.

GOD is infinite. 1 Kings 8:23 LORD God of Israel, there is no God like You in heaven above or on earth below,

GOD is one. Deuteronomy 6:4 The LORD our God, the LORD is One.

GOD is omnipresent. Psalms 139:7-12 Where can I go to escape Your Spirit? Where can I flee from Your presence? If I go up to heaven, You are there; if I make my bed in Sheol, You are there. If I live at the eastern horizon or settle at the western limits, even there Your hand will lead me; Your right hand will hold on to me. If I say, "Surely the darkness will hide me, and the light around me will be night" — even the darkness is not dark to You. The night shines like the day; darkness and light are alike to You.

GOD is omnipotent. Genesis 18:14 Is anything impossible for the LORD?

GOD is omniscient. Psalms 147:5 Our Lord is great, vast in power;
His understanding is infinite.

GOD is immutable. Hebrews 1:10-12 In the beginning, Lord,
You established the earth, and the heavens are the works of Your hands; they will perish, but You remain. They will all wear out-like clothing; You will roll them up like a cloak, and they will be changed like a robe. But You are the same, and Your years will never end. In the beginning, Lord, You established the earth, and the heavens are the works of Your hands; they will

perish, but You remain. They will all wear out like clothing; You will roll them up like a cloak, and they will be changed like a robe. But You are the same, and Your years will never end.

GOD is incomprehensible. Job 5:7-9 But mankind is born for trouble as surely as sparks fly upward. However, if I were you, I would appeal to God and would present my case to Him. He does great and unsearchable things, wonders without number.

GOD is inscrutable. Romans 11:33 Oh, the depth of the riches both of the wisdom and the knowledge of God! How unsearchable His judgments and untraceable His ways!

GOD is righteous and just. Exodus 9:27 Pharaoh sent for Moses and Aaron. "I have sinned this time," he said to them. "Yahweh is the Righteous One, and I and my people are the guilty ones.

GOD is holy. Leviticus 19:2 Speak to the entire Israelite community and tell them: Be holy because I, Yahweh your God, am holy.

GOD is wise. Psalms136:5 He made the heavens skillfully.

GOD is true. Titus 1:1,2 Paul, a slave of God and an apostle of Jesus Christ, to build up the faith of God's elect and their knowledge of the truth that leads to godliness, in the hope of eternal life that God, who cannot lie, promised before time began.

GOD is faithful. Deuteronomy 7:9 Know that Yahweh your God is God, the faithful God who keeps His gracious covenant loyalty for a thousand generations with those who love Him and keep His commands.

GOD is good. Romans 2:4 Or do you despise the riches of His kindness, restraint, and patience, not recognizing that God's kindness is intended to lead you to repentance?

GOD is gracious. Psalms 111:4 He has caused His wonderful works to be remembered. The LORD is gracious and compassionate.

GOD is Love. Deuteronomy 7:8 But because the LORD loved you and kept the oath He swore to your fathers,

GOD is merciful. Psalms 103:8-17 The LORD is compassionate and gracious, slow to anger and rich in faithful love. He will not always accuse us or be angry forever. He has not dealt with us as our sins deserve or repaid us according to our offenses. For as high as the heavens are above the earth, so great is His faithful love toward those who fear Him. As far as the east is from the west, so far has He removed our transgressions from us. As a father has compassion on his children, so the LORD has compassion on those who fear Him.

GOD is a living GOD. Psalms 84:2 I long and yearn for the courts of the LORD; my heart and flesh cry out for the living God.

GOD is distinct from His creation and above it. Genesis 1:1 In the beginning God created the heavens and the earth.

GOD is above the universe He created. Isaiah 40:22, 57:15

GOD is Immutable. Psalms 102:25-27 Long ago You established the earth, and the heavens are the work of Your hands. They will perish, but You will endure; all of them will wear out like clothing. You will change them like a garment, and they will pass away. But You are the same, and Your years will never end.

GOD is inscrutable. Romans 11:33 Oh, the depth of the riches both of the wisdom and the knowledge of God! How unsearchable His judgments and untraceable His ways!

GOD is Incomprehensible. Isaiah 46:9 Remember what happened long ago, for I am God, and there is no other; I am God, and no one is like Me.

GOD is the eternal, everlasting GOD. Psalms 90:2 Before the mountains were born, Or You gave birth to the earth and the world, even from everlasting to everlasting, You are God.

The Trinity Of God

"There is one GOD, but in the unity of the GODHEAD there are three eternal and co-equal Persons, the same in substance, but distinct in subsistence." (C.C. Ryrie)

GOD is one – Isaiah 44:6 This is what the LORD, the King of Israel and its Redeemer, the LORD of Hosts, says: I am the first and I am the last. There is no God but Me. Yet GOD is three in one.

The Father, Son and Holy Spirit are distinct persons –
John 14:16 And I will ask the Father, and He will give you another Counselor to be with you forever.
John 14:26 But the Counselor, the Holy Spirit — the Father will send Him in My name — will teach you all things and remind you of everything I have told you.
John 15:26 When the Counselor comes, the One I will send to you from the Father — the Spirit of truth who proceeds from the Father — He will testify about Me.

BIBLE DOCTRINE

GOD is FATHER and Father is YAHWEH – Hebrews 5:5 In the same way, the Messiah did not exalt Himself to become a high priest, but the One who said to Him, You are My Son; today I have become Your Father,

GOD is SON and SON is YAHWEH – John 8:58 Jesus said to them, "I assure you: Before Abraham was, I am."

GOD is HOLY SPIRIT and HOLY SPIRIT is YAHWEH – Acts 28:25-26 Disagreeing among themselves, they began to leave after Paul made one statement: "The Holy Spirit correctly spoke through the prophet Isaiah to your ancestors when He said, Go to these people and say: You will listen and listen, yet never understand; and you will look and look, yet never perceive.

BIBLE DOCTRINE

DOCTRINE OF JESUS CHRIST

Before we look at Christology we need to answer the most important question ever asked in all history, that is found in John 8:29 Jesus asked the question, 'Who do you say that I am?'

We Say That;
All things were created through Christ - John 1:3 All things were created through Him, and apart from Him not one thing was created that has been created.

Jesus Christ is the Son of the past - Colossians 1:15 He is the image of the invisible God, the firstborn over all creation

Jesus Christ is the Son of the present - Colossians 1:18 He is also the head of the body, the church; He is the beginning, the firstborn from the dead, so that He might come to have first place in everything.

Jesus Christ is the Son of the future - Matthew 16:27 For the Son of Man is going to come with His angels in the glory of His Father, and then He will reward each according to what he has done.

FOUNDATIONS OF FAITH

Jesus Christ is the Son of the eternal - John 1:18 No one has ever seen God. The One and Only Son — the One who is at the Father's side — He has revealed Him.

Jesus is 100% the son of man - Matthew 8:20 Jesus told him, "Foxes have dens and birds of the sky have nests, but the Son of Man has no place to lay His head."

Christ is 100% the Son of GOD - Matthew 16:16 "You are the Messiah, the Son of the living God!"

Christ is God the Son, the second person of the Trinity - John 1:1 In the beginning was the Word, and the Word was with God, and the Word was God.

Christ is The Word of God - Matthew 4:4 Man must not live on bread alone but on every word that comes from the mouth of God."

Christ was with The Father and The Holy Spirit before all ages - John 10:30 The Father and I are one.

Christ is the light of the world - John 8:12 I am the light of the world.

Christ is the true God of true God - 1 Corinthians 8:6 yet for us there is one God, the Father. All things are from Him, and we exist for Him. And there is one Lord, Jesus Christ. All things are through Him, and we exist through Him. Christ is begotten not made - John 3:16 For God loved the world in this way: He gave His One and Only Son, so that everyone who believes in Him will not perish but have eternal life.

Christ is of one substance with the Father, through whom all things were made - Colossians 1:16 For everything was created by Him, in heaven and on earth, the visible and the invisible, whether thrones or dominions or rulers or authorities — all things have been created through Him and for Him.

Christ was born as Jesus through the virgin Mary, His earthly mother - Isaiah 7:14 Therefore, the Lord Himself will give you a sign: The virgin will conceive, have a son, and name him Immanuel.

Christ was sent from the heavens to earth for our salvation and was made flesh by the power of the Holy Spirit - John 6:38 For I have come down from heaven, not to do My will, but the will of Him who sent Me.

Christ is the bread of Life - John 6: 35 I am the bread of life," Jesus told them. "No one who comes to Me will ever be hungry, and no one who believes in Me will ever be thirsty again.

Jesus is the only man ever to have lived a sinless life - 1 Peter 2:22 He did not commit sin, and no deceit was found in His mouth;

Jesus Christ was despised by his own people, was crucified for us under Pontius Pilate, died and was buried, and rose again on the third day, ascended into the heavens to sit on the right hand of the Father - Matthew 27:22-56 Pilate asked them, "What should I do then with Jesus, who is called Messiah?" They all answered, "Crucify Him!" Then he said, "Why? What has He done wrong?" But they kept shouting, "Crucify Him!" all the more. When Pilate saw that he was getting nowhere, but that a riot was starting instead, he took some water, washed his hands in front of the crowd, and said, "I am innocent of this man's blood. See to it yourselves!" All the people answered, "His blood be on us and on our children!" Then he released Barabbas to them. But after having Jesus flogged, he handed Him over to be crucified. Then the governor's soldiers took Jesus into headquarters and gathered the whole company around Him. They stripped Him and dressed Him in a scarlet military robe. They twisted together a crown of thorns, put it on His head, and placed a reed in His right hand. And they knelt down before Him and mocked Him: "Hail, King of the Jews!" Then they spit on Him, took the reed, and kept hitting Him on the head. When they had mocked Him, they stripped Him of the robe, put His clothes on Him, and led Him away to crucify Him. As they were going out, they found a Cyrenian man named Simon. They forced this man to carry His cross. When they came to a place called Golgotha (which means Skull Place), they gave Him wine mixed with gall to drink. But when He tasted it, He would not drink it. After crucifying Him they divided His clothes by casting lots. Then they sat down and were guarding Him there. Above His head they put up the charge against Him in writing: THIS IS JESUS THE KING OF THE JEWS.

Then two criminals were crucified with Him, one on the right and one on the left. Those who passed by were yelling insults at Him, shaking their heads and saying, "The One who would demolish the sanctuary and rebuild it in three days, save Yourself! If You are the Son of God, come down from the cross!" In the same way the chief priests, with the scribes and elders, mocked Him and said, "He saved others, but He cannot save Himself! He is the King of Israel! Let Him come down now from the cross, and we will believe in Him. He has put His trust in God; let God rescue Him now — if He wants Him! For He said, 'I am God's Son.'" In the same way even the criminals who were crucified with Him kept taunting Him. From noon until three in the afternoon darkness came over the whole land. About three in the afternoon Jesus cried out with a loud voice, " Elí, Elí, lemá sabachtháni?" that is, " My God, My God, why have You forsaken Me?" When some of those standing there heard this, they said, "He's calling for Elijah!" Immediately one of them ran and got a sponge, filled it with sour wine, fixed it on a reed, and offered Him a drink. But the rest said, "Let's see if Elijah comes to save Him!" Jesus shouted again with a loud voice and gave up His spirit. Suddenly, the curtain of the sanctuary was split in two from top to bottom; the earth quaked and the rocks were split. The tombs were also opened and many bodies of the saints who had fallen asleep were raised.

And they came out of the tombs after His resurrection, entered the holy city, and appeared to many. When the centurion and those with him, who were guarding Jesus, saw the earthquake and the things that had happened, they were terrified and said, "This man really was God's Son!"

Many women who had followed Jesus from Galilee and ministered to Him were there, looking on from a distance. Among them were Mary Magdalene, Mary the mother of James and Joseph, and the mother of Zebedee's sons.

Jesus died on the cross for humankind and thus atoned for our sins through the shedding of His blood.

Romans 5:12-17 Therefore, just as sin entered the world through one man, and death through sin, in this way death spread to all men, because all sinned. In fact, sin was in the world before the law, but sin is not charged to a person's account when there is no law. Nevertheless, death reigned from Adam to Moses, even over those who did not sin in the likeness of Adam's transgression. He is a prototype of the Coming One. But the gift is not like the trespass. For if by the one man's trespass the many died, how much more have the grace of God and the gift overflowed to the many by the grace of the one man, Jesus Christ. And the gift is not like the one man's sin, because from one sin came the judgment, resulting in condemnation, but from many trespasses came the gift, resulting in justification. Since by the one man's trespass, death reigned through that one man, how much more will those who receive the overflow of grace and the gift of righteousness reign in life through the one man, Jesus Christ.

Jesus rose from the dead on the third day, ascended to the right hand of the Father, and will return again in power and glory.

Ephesians 1:20 He demonstrated this power in the Messiah by raising Him from the dead and seating Him at His right hand in the heavens.

Jesus Christ is the only way to the Father and He alone offers remission of sins and resurrection of the flesh and life everlasting. John 3:16 For God loved the world in this way: He gave His One and Only Son, so that everyone who believes in Him will not perish but have eternal life.

What Jesus Christ Means To People Across Varied Professions:

To the artist, He is the source of their creativity. Exodus 35:31,32 He has filled him with God's Spirit, with wisdom, understanding, and ability in every kind of craft to design artistic works in gold, silver, and bronze,

To the architect, He is the Chief Cornerstone. 1 Peter 2:6 Look! I lay a stone in Zion, a chosen and honored cornerstone, and the one who believes in Him will never be put to shame!

To the astronomer, He is the Sun of Righteousness. Malachi 4:2 But for you who fear My name, the sun of righteousness will rise with healing in its wings,

To the baker, He is the Bread of Life. John 6:35 I am the bread of life," Jesus told them. "No one who comes to Me will ever be hungry, and no one who believes in Me will ever be thirsty again.

To the banker, is the Hidden Treasure. Isaiah 28:16 Therefore the Lord GOD said: "Look, I have laid a stone in Zion, a tested stone, a precious cornerstone, a sure foundation; the one who believes will be unshakable.

To the investor, he gives the financial advice. Matthew 25:27 'then you should have deposited my money with the bankers. And when I returned I would have received my money back with interest.'

To the biologist, He is life. Romans 8:22 The whole creation has been groaning together in the pains of childbirth until now.

To the builder, He is the sure foundation is the sure foundation. Isaiah 28:16 Therefore the Lord GOD said: "Look, I have laid a stone in Zion, a tested stone, a precious cornerstone, a sure foundation; the one who believes will be unshakable.

To the carpenter, He is the Door. John 10:7 I assure you: I am the door of the sheep.

To the doctor, He is the great Physician. Jeremiah 8:22 Is there no balm in Gilead? Is there no physician there? So why has the healing of my dear people not come about?

To the educator, He is the New and the Living Way. Hebrews 10:20 by a new and living way He has opened for us through the curtain (that is, His flesh),

To the farmer is The Lord of the harvest. Luke 10:20 Therefore, pray to the Lord of the harvest to send out workers into His harvest."

To the florist, He is the rose of Sharon, and the lily of the valley. Song of Songs 2:1 I am a rose of Sharon, a lily of the valleys.

To the Geologist, He is the rock of ages. 1 Corinthians 10:4 and all drank the same spiritual drink. For they drank from a spiritual rock that followed them, and that rock was Christ.

To the horticulturist, He is the true vine. John 15:5 I am the vine; you are the branches. The one who remains in Me and I in him produces much fruit, because you can do nothing without Me.

To the judge, He is the lawgiver. Isaiah 33:22 For the LORD is our Judge, the LORD is our lawgiver, the LORD is our King. He will save us.

To the lawyer, He is an advocate. 1 John 2:1,2 My little children, I am writing you these things so that you may not sin. But if anyone does sin, we have an advocate with the Father — Jesus Christ the Righteous One. He Himself is the propitiation for our sins, and not only for ours, but also for those of the whole world.

To the laborer, He is the giver. Deuteronomy 28:12 The LORD will open for you His abundant storehouse, the sky, to give your land rain in its season and to bless all the work of your hands. You will lend to many nations, but you will not borrow.

To the news-anchor, He is the good news. Romans 10:15 How beautiful are the feet of those who announce the gospel of good things!

To the mason, He is the Chief Cornerstone. Matthew. 21:42 The stone that the builders rejected has become the cornerstone.

To the psychologist, He is the counselor. Isaiah 9:6 For a child will be born for us, a son will be given to us, and the government will be on His shoulders. He will be named Wonderful Counselor, Mighty God, Eternal Father, Prince of Peace.

To the philosopher, He is the wisdom of God. 1 Corinthians 1:20 Where is the philosopher? Where is the scholar? Where is the debater of this age? Hasn't God made the world's wisdom foolish?

To the preacher, He is the word of God. 1 Corinthians 1:24 Yet to those who are called, both Jews and Greeks, Christ is God's power and God's wisdom,

To the servant, He is the good master. Luke 9:38 Master, I beg You to look at my son, because he's my only child.

To the statesmen, He is the desire of all nations. Haggai 2:7 I will shake all the nations so that the treasures of all the nations will come, and I will fill this house with glory,

To the student, He is the teacher. John 13:13 You call Me Teacher and Lord. This is well said, for I am.

To the lover, he is the greatest love all. Song of Songs 2:1 Oh, that he would kiss me with the kisses of his mouth! For your love is more delightful than wine.

To the theologian, He is the author and finisher of our faith. Hebrews 12:2 keeping our eyes on Jesus, the source and perfecter of our faith,

And most of all, to the sinner, He is the lamb of God, who takes away the sin of the world, to the Christian, He is the Son of the Living God. John 1:29 Here is the Lamb of God, who takes away the sin of the world!

The Son Of God In The Old Testament:

Genesis	He has the seed of the woman and Shiloh.
Exodus	He is the pass-over of the lamb.
Leviticus	He is the anointed high priest.
Numbers	He is the star of Jacob and the brazen serpent.

BIBLE DOCTRINE

Deuteronomy	He is the Great Rock.
Joshua	He is the captain of the Lord of Hosts.
Judges	He is the messenger of Jehovah.
Ruth	He is the kinsman redeemer.
1 Samuel	He is a great judge.
2 Samuel	He is the seed of David.
1 kings	He is Lord God of Israel.
2 kings	He is the God of the Cherubim.
1 Chronicles	He is the God of our salvation.
2 Chronicles	He is the God of our fathers.
Ezra	He is the Lord of heaven and earth.
Nehemiah	He is a covenant keeping God.
Esther	He is the God of Providence.
Job	He has that risen and returning Redeemer.
Psalm	He has anointed Son and the king of Glory.
Proverbs	He is the wisdom of God.
Ecclesiastes	He is the One above the sun.
Song of Solomon	He is altogether lovely.
Isaiah	He is Emmanuel, Wonderful, Counselor, Mighty God, Everlasting Father, Prince of Peace, Righteousness, Righteous Servant and the Man of Sorrows.
Jeremiah	He is The Lord our Righteousness.
Lamentations	He is the faithful and compassionate God.
Ezekiel	He is the Lord who is there.

FOUNDATIONS OF FAITH

Daniel	He is the smiting stone, the Son of God, and the Son of man.
Hosea	He is the King of the resurrection.
Joel	He is the God of the battle and the giver of the Spirit.
Amos	He is God of Hosts and He is the God of the plumb-line.
Obediah	He is the destroyer of the proud.
Jonah	He is the risen Prophet, God of the second choice, and the long-suffering one.
Micah	He is the God of Jacob, the God of Bethlehem and the pardoning God.
Nahum	He is the avenging God and the bringer of good tidings.
Habakkuk	He is the everlasting glorious and anointed one.
Zephaniah	He is the king of Israel.
Haggai	He is the desire of all nations.
Zechariah	He is the Branch, builder of the temple, King of the triumphal entry, the pierced one, and the King of the earth.
Malachi	He is the Lord of remembrance.

The Son Of God In The New Testament:

Matthew	He is King of the Jews.
Mark	He is servant.
Luke	He is the perfect man.
John	He is eternal God.
Acts	He is Ascended Lord.

BIBLE DOCTRINE

Romans	He is the Lord our righteousness.
1 Corinthians	He is our resurrection.
2 Corinthians	He is God of all comfort.
Galatians	He is the Redeemer from the devil.
Ephesians	He is the Head of the Church.
Philippians	He is the supplier of all needs.
Colossians	He is the fullness of the Godhead.
1 Thessalonians	He is the coming Christ.
2 Thessalonians	He is the consuming Christ.
1 Timothy	He is the mediator and savior of sinners.
2 Timothy	He is the Righteous and rewarding judge and author of scripture.
Titus	He is our great God and Savior.
Philemon	He is the payer of our debt.
Hebrews	He is appointed heir of all things.
Hebrews	He is One better than the prophets and the angels.
Hebrews	He is the Captain of our salvation.
Hebrews	He is our Merciful and faithful high priest.
Hebrews	He is our Great intercessor.
Hebrews	He is our Mediator of the new covenant.
Hebrews	He is our Good shepherd of the sheep.
James	He is ever present God, great physician and the one who is coming.

1 Peter	He is the unblemished lamb, great example, Good Shepard and Lord of glory.
2 Peter	He is the beloved son.
1 John	He is the Word of Life, Advocate, Propitiation, and the Son of God.
2 John	He is the Son of the Father.
3 John	He is the truth.
Jude	He is the preserver and only wise God.
Revelation	He is the Alpha and the Omega, the Lion of Judah, He slain and resurrected lamb, He is the king of kings, and He is the bright and morning star.

Theophanies And Christophanies

The Old Testament ministry of Christ is called a Christophany, while a Theophanies is a pre-Bethlehem appearance of God.

In Greek theophanies is divided into two words. One is Theos, which in Greek is God, and phaino is where we get the word 'phanies' which means to appear, where a Christophanies is Christ's appearance, pre-Bethlehem.

So a theophany is an appearance of God. And a Christophany is an appearance of Christ. Let me give some examples.

A Theophanies and a Christophanies show that the heart of God is to be physically and visibly and inseparably present with His people, and single purpose is to restore His people to God.

The Christophanies always appeared in a visible pillar of cloud by day and a pillar of fire by night and led His people through the wilderness and (we are told) "did not depart from them" is the same Christ who says, in the New Testament, "I am with you always."

Some Old Testament Theophanies:

The Angel of the Lord appeared to Hagar, Abraham's Egyptian wife. Genesis 16:7 The Angel of the LORD found her by a spring of water in the wilderness, the spring on the way to Shur.

The Angel of the Lord appeared to Abraham. Genesis 18:10 the LORD said, "I will certainly come back to you in about a year's time, and your wife Sarah will have a son!" Now Sarah was listening at the entrance of the tent behind him.

The Angel of the Lord appeared to Jacob. Genesis 28:12-15 And he dreamed: A stairway was set on the ground with its top reaching heaven, and God's angels were going up and down on it. Yahweh was standing there beside him, saying, "I am Yahweh, the God of your father Abraham and the God of Isaac. I will give you and your offspring the land that you are now sleeping on. Your offspring will be like the dust of the earth, and you will spread out toward the west, the east, the north, and the south. All the peoples on earth will be blessed through you and your offspring. Look, I am with you and will watch over you wherever you go. I will bring you back to this land, for I will not leave you until I have done what I have promised you."

The Angel of the Lord appeared to Moses. Exodus 3:4,5 When the LORD saw that he had gone over to look, God called out to him from the bush, "Moses, Moses!" "Here I am," he answered. "Do not come closer," He said. "Remove the sandals from your feet, for the place where you are standing is holy ground."

The Angel of the Lord appeared to Joshua. Joshua 5:13-15 When Joshua was near Jericho, he looked up and saw a man standing in front of him with a drawn sword in His hand. Joshua approached Him and asked, "Are You for us or for our enemies?" "Neither," He replied. "I have now come as commander of the LORD'S army." Then Joshua bowed with his face to the ground in worship and asked Him, "What does my Lord want to say to His servant?" The commander of the LORD'S army said to Joshua, "Remove the sandals from your feet, for the place where you are standing is holy." And Joshua did so.

The Angel of the Lord appeared to Gideon. Judges 6:12 Then the Angel of the LORD appeared to him and said:

The Angel of the Lord appeared to Samson's parents. Judges 13:3 The Angel of the LORD appeared to the woman and said to her, "It is true that you are unable to conceive and have no children, but you will conceive and give birth to a son.

The Angel of the Lord appeared to Shadrack, Meshack, and Abednego in the fiery furnace. Daniel 3:25 "Look! I see four men, not tied, walking around in the fire unharmed; and the fourth looks like a son of the gods."

The Angel of the Lord appeared to Daniel. Daniel 6:22 My God sent His angel and shut the lions' mouths. They haven't hurt me, for I was found innocent before Him. Also, I have not committed a crime against you my king."

The Angel of the Lord appeared to Zechariah. Zechariah 1:9 I asked, "What are these, my lord?"

The angel who was talking to me replied, "I will show you what they are."

In the Old Testament we have man (The 1st Adam) made in the image of God and in the New Testament we see God revealed in the image of man (The 2nd Adam / Jesus).

The Virgin Birth Incarnation

False views concerning the virgin birth of Jesus are all refuted by John 1:1 In the beginning was the Word and the Word was with God, and the Word was God.

The correct Biblical view concerning the virgin birth of Jesus is best said by A.H. Strong, Systematic Theology, p. 673. "In one person Jesus Christ, there are two natures, a human nature and a divine nature, each in its completeness and integrity, and these two natures are organically and indissolubly united, yet so that no third nature is formed."

Jesus is 100% man born of the virgin Mary and yet He is 100% Christ the Son of God, sent from God to be born of the virgin Mary.

Prophecies Concerning The Virgin Birth:

Through Isaiah. Isaiah 7:14 Therefore, the Lord Himself will give you a sign: The virgin will conceive, have a son, and name him Immanuel.

Through Micah. Micah 5:2 Bethlehem Ephrathah, you are small among the clans of Judah; One will come from you to be ruler over Israel for Me. His origin is from antiquity, from eternity.

To Zacharias. Luke 1:17 And he will go before Him in the spirit and power of Elijah, to turn the hearts of fathers to their children, and the disobedient to the understanding of the righteous, to make ready for the Lord a prepared people.

To Mary. Luke 1:31 Now listen: You will conceive and give birth to a son, and you will call His name Jesus.

To Elizabeth. Luke 1:42 Then she exclaimed with a loud cry: "You are the most blessed of women, and your child will be blessed!

To Joseph. Matthew 1:20,21 After he had considered these things, an angel of the Lord suddenly appeared to him in a dream, saying, "Joseph, son of David, don't be afraid to take Mary as your wife, because what has been conceived in her is by the Holy Spirit. She will give birth to a son, and you are to name Him Jesus because He will save His people from their sins."

To the Shepherds. Luke 2:10-12 But the angel said to them, "Don't be afraid, for look, I proclaim to you good news of great joy that will be for all the people: Today a Savior, who is Messiah the Lord, was born for you in the city of David. This will be the sign for you: You will find a baby wrapped snugly in cloth and lying in a feeding trough."

To the Wise Men. Matthew 2:1,2 After Jesus was born in Bethlehem of Judea in the days of King Herod, wise men from the east arrived unexpectedly in Jerusalem, saying, "Where is He who has been born King of the Jews? For we saw His star in the east and have come to worship Him."

To Simeon. Luke 2:25-32 There was a man in Jerusalem whose name was Simeon. This man was righteous and devout, looking forward to Israel's consolation, and the Holy Spirit was on him. It had been revealed to him by the Holy Spirit that he would not see death before he saw the Lord's Messiah. Guided by the Spirit, he entered the temple complex. When the parents brought in the child Jesus to perform for Him what was customary under the law, Simeon took Him up in his arms, praised God, and said: Now, Master, You can dismiss Your slave in peace, as You promised. For my eyes have seen Your salvation. You have prepared it in the presence of all peoples — a light for revelation to the Gentiles and glory to Your people Israel.

To Anna Luke 2:38 At that very moment, she came up and began to thank God and to speak about Him to all who were looking forward to the redemption of Jerusalem.

Reasons For The Virgin Birth.

To reveal the invisible God. John 1:18 No one has ever seen God. The One and Only Son — the One who is at the Father's side — He has revealed Him.

To fulfill prophecy. Genesis 3:15 I will put hostility between you and the woman, and between your seed and her seed. He will strike your head, and you will strike his heel.

To ensure the Davidic covenant. 2 Samuel 7:12-16 When your time comes and you rest with your fathers, I will raise up after you your descendant, who will come from your body, and I will establish his kingdom. He will build a house for My name, and I will establish the throne of his kingdom forever. I will be a father to him, and he will be a son to Me. When he does wrong, I will discipline him with a human rod and with blows from others. But My faithful love will never leave him as I removed it from Saul; I removed him from your way. Your house and kingdom will endure before Me forever, and your throne will be established forever.'"

To make a sacrifice for our sins. Hebrews 2:9 But we do see Jesus — made lower than the angels for a short time so that by God's grace He might taste death for everyone — crowned with glory and honor because of His suffering in death.

To reconcile man to God. 2 Corinthians 5:19 That is, in Christ, God was reconciling the world to Himself, not counting their trespasses against them, and He has committed the message of reconciliation to us.

To provide an example for believers. 1 Peter 2:21 For you were called to this, because Christ also suffered for you, leaving you an example, so that you should follow in His steps.

To provide the believer with a high priest. Hebrewsm2:17 Therefore, He had to be like His brothers in every way, so that He could become a merciful and faithful high priest in service to God, to make propitiation for the sins of the people.

To destroy the devil and his works. Hebrews 2:14 Now since the children have flesh and blood in common, Jesus also shared in these, so that through His death He might destroy the one holding the power of death — that is, the Devil

BIBLE DOCTRINE

Biblical Names And Titles Of Jesus Christ

A Living Stone. 1 Peter 2:4 Coming to Him, a living stone — rejected by men but chosen and valuable to God

The last Adam. 1 Corinthians 15:45 So it is written: The first man Adam became a living being; the last Adam became a life-giving Spirit.

Advocate. 1 John 2:1 But if anyone does sin, we have an advocate with the Father — Jesus Christ the Righteous One.

Alpha and the Omega. Revelation 1:8 "I am the Alpha and the Omega," says the Lord God, "the One who is, who was, and who is coming, the Almighty."

Anointed. Acts 4:27 "For, in fact, in this city both Herod and Pontius Pilate, with the Gentiles and the people of Israel, assembled together against Your holy Servant Jesus, whom You anointed,

Author and Finisher of Faith. Hebrews 12:2 keeping our eyes on Jesus, the source and perfecter of our faith, who for the joy that lay before Him endured a cross and despised the shame and has sat down at the right hand of God's throne.

Author of Salvation. Hebrews 5:9 After He was perfected, He became the source of eternal salvation for all who obey Him,

Brightness of his Glory. Hebrews 1:3 The Son is the radiance of God's glory and the exact expression of His nature, sustaining all things by His powerful word. After making purification for sins, He sat down at the right hand of the Majesty on high.

Chief Shepherd. 1 Peter 5:4 And when the chief Shepherd appears, you will receive the unfading crown of glory.

Counselor. Isaiah 9:6 For a child will be born for us, a son will be given to us, and the government will be on His shoulders. He will be named Wonderful Counselor, Mighty God, Eternal Father, Prince of Peace.

Deliverer. Romans 11:26 The Liberator will come from Zion; He will turn away godlessness from Jacob.

Emanuel. Matthew 1:23 See, the virgin will become pregnant and give birth to a son, and they will name Him Immanuel, which is translated "God is with us."

Eternal Life. 1 John 5:20 And we know that the Son of God has come and has given us understanding so that we may know the true One. We are in the true One — that is, in His Son Jesus Christ. He is the true God and eternal life.

Everlasting Father. Isaiah 9:6 For a child will be born for us, a son will be given to us, and the government will be on His shoulders. He will be named Wonderful Counselor, Mighty God, Eternal Father, Prince of Peace.

Everlasting God. Isaiah 40:28 Do you not know? Have you not heard? Yahweh is the everlasting God, the Creator of the whole earth. He never grows faint or weary; there is no limit to His understanding.

Faithful and True. Revelation 19:11 Its rider is called Faithful and True, and He judges and makes war in righteousness.

Faithful Witness. Revelation 1:5 Jesus Christ, the faithful witness, the firstborn from the dead and the ruler of the kings of the earth.

Gift of God. John 4:10 "If you knew the gift of God, and who is saying to you, 'Give Me a drink,' you would ask Him, and He would give you living water."

God my Savior. Luke 1:47 and my spirit has rejoiced in God my Savior,

God with Us. Matthew 1:23 See, the virgin will become pregnant and give birth to a son, and they will name Him Immanuel, which is translated "God is with us."

Great Shepherd. Hebrews 13:20 Now may the God of peace, who brought up from the dead our Lord Jesus — the great Shepherd of the sheep — with the blood of the everlasting covenant,

He that Liveth. Revelation 1:18 and the Living One. I was dead, but look — I am alive forever and ever, and I hold the keys of death and Hades.

Hidden Manna. Revelation 2:17 "Anyone who has an ear should listen to what the Spirit says to the churches. I will give the victor some of the hidden manna. I will also give him a white stone, and on the stone a new name is inscribed that no one knows except the one who receives it.

High Priest. Hebrews 4:14 Therefore, since we have a great high priest who has passed through the heavens — Jesus the Son of God — let us hold fast to the confession

Holy One of God. Mark 1:24 What do You have to do with us, Jesus — Nazarene? Have You come to destroy us? I know who You are — the Holy One of God!"

Horn of Salvation. Luke 1:69 He has raised up a horn of salvation for us in the house of His servant David,

I AM. John 8:24 For if you do not believe that I am He, you will die in your sins.

I AM Bread of Life. John 6:35 "I am the bread of life," Jesus told them.

I AM Light of the World. John 8:12 "I am the light of the world. Anyone who follows Me will never walk in the darkness but will have the light of life."

I AM the Good Shepherd. John 10:11 I am the good shepherd. The good shepherd lays down his life for the sheep.

I AM the Door. John 10:9 I am the door. If anyone enters by Me, he will be saved and will come in and go out and find pasture.

I AM the Resurrection. John 11:25 I am the resurrection and the life. The one who believes in Me, even if he dies, will live.

I AM The True Vine. John 15:5 I am the vine; you are the branches. The one who remains in Me and I in him produces much fruit, because you can do nothing without Me.

I AM the Way. John 14:6 I am the way, the truth, and the life. No one comes to the Father except through Me.

I AM the Truth. John 1:14 The Word became flesh and took up residence among us. We observed His glory, the glory as the One and Only Son from the Father, full of grace and truth.
Image of God. 2 Corinthians 4:4 ...they cannot see the light of the gospel of the glory of Christ, who is the image of God.

Jesus. Matthew 1:1 The historical record of Jesus Christ, the Son of David, the Son of Abraham:

Judge. Acts 17:31 because He has set a day when He is going to judge the world in righteousness by the Man He has appointed. He has provided proof of this to everyone by raising Him from the dead."

Jehovah. Isaiah 26:4 Trust in the LORD forever, because in Yah, the LORD, is an everlasting rock!

King of Israel. Matthew. 27:42 He saved others, but He cannot save Himself! He is the King of Israel! Let Him come down now from the cross, and we will believe in Him.

King of kings. Revelation 17:14 These will make war against the Lamb, but the Lamb will conquer them because He is Lord of lords and King of kings. Those with Him are called, chosen, and faithful.

Lamb of God. John 1:29 Here is the Lamb of God, who takes away the sin of the world!

Lawgiver. Isaiah 33:22 For the LORD is our Judge, the LORD is our lawgiver, the LORD is our King. He will save us.

Lily of the Valleys. Song of Songs 2:1 I am a rose of Sharon, a lily of the valleys.

Lion of the Tribe of Judah. Revelation 5:5 Then one of the elders said to me, "Stop crying. Look! The Lion from the tribe of Judah, the Root of David, has been victorious so that He may open the scroll and its seven seals."

Lord. Romans 10:13 For everyone who calls on the name of the Lord will be saved.

Lord God Almighty. Revelation 4:8 Holy, holy, holy, Lord God, the Almighty, who was, who is, and who is coming.

Lord of All. Acts 10:36 He sent the message to the Israelites, proclaiming the good news of peace through Jesus Christ — He is Lord of all.

Lord of Glory. 1 Corinthians 2:8 None of the rulers of this age knew this wisdom, for if they had known it, they would not have crucified the Lord of glory.

Lord of the Sabbath. Luke 6:5 "The Son of Man is Lord of the Sabbath."

Man. Acts 17:31 because He has set a day when He is going to judge the world in righteousness by the Man He has appointed. He has provided proof of this to everyone by raising Him from the dead.

Man from Heaven. 1 Corinthians 15:48 Like the man made of dust, so are those who are made of dust; like the heavenly man,

Master John 13:13 You call Me Teacher and Lord. This is well said, for I am.

Mediator of the New Covenant. Hebrews 9:15 Therefore, He is the mediator of a new covenant, so that those who are called might receive the promise of the eternal inheritance, because a death has taken place for redemption from the transgressions committed under the first covenant.

Messiah. John 1:41 He first found his own brother Simon and told him, "We have found the Messiah!" (which means "Anointed One"),

Mighty God. Isaiah 9:6 For a child will be born for us, a son will be given to us, and the government will be on His shoulders. He will be named Wonderful Counselor, Mighty God, Eternal Father, Prince of Peace.

Morning Star. Revelation 22:16 I, Jesus, have sent My angel to attest these things to you for the churches. I am the Root and the Offspring of David, the Bright Morning Star.

Nazarene. Matthew 2:23 Then he went and settled in a town called Nazareth to fulfill what was spoken through the prophets, that He will be called a Nazarene.

Our Husband. 2 Corinthians 11:2 For I am jealous over you with a godly jealousy, because I have promised you in marriage to one husband — to present a pure virgin to Christ.

Only begotten Son. John 1:18 No one has ever seen God.
The One and Only Son — the One who is at the Father's side — He has revealed Him.

Passover. 1 Corinthians 5:7 Clean out the old yeast so that you may be a new batch. You are indeed unleavened, for Christ our Passover has been sacrificed.

Physician. Matthew 9:12 But when He heard this, He said, "Those who are well don't need a doctor, but the sick do.

Potentate. 1 Timothy 6:15 God will bring this about in His own time. He is the blessed and only Sovereign, the King of kings, and the Lord of lords,

Power of God. 1 Corinthians 1:24 Yet to those who are called, both Jews and Greeks, Christ is God's power and God's wisdom,

Priest. Hebrews 4:14 Therefore, since we have a great high priest who has passed through the heavens — Jesus the Son of God — let us hold fast to the confession.

Prince of Life. Acts 3:15 You killed the source of life, whom God raised from the dead; we are witnesses of this.

Prince of Peace. Isaiah 9:6 For a child will be born for us, a son will be given to us, and the government will be on His shoulders. He will be named Wonderful Counselor, Mighty God, Eternal Father, Prince of Peace.

Propitiation. 1 John 2:2 He Himself is the propitiation for our sins, and not only for ours, but also for those of the whole world.

Prophet. Acts 3:22 Moses said: The Lord your God will raise up for you a Prophet like me from among your brothers. You must listen to Him in everything He will say to you.

Rabbi. John 3:2 This man came to Him at night and said, "Rabbi, we know that You have come from God as a teacher, for no one could perform these signs You do unless God were with him."

Ransom. 1 Timothy 2:6 who gave Himself — a ransom for all, a testimony at the proper time.

Reaper. Revelation 14:15 Another angel came out of the sanctuary, crying out in a loud voice to the One who was seated on the cloud, "Use your sickle and reap, for the time to reap has come, since the harvest of the earth is ripe."

Redeemer. Isaiah 59:20 "The Redeemer will come to Zion, and to those in Jacob who turn from transgression."

Refiner. Malachi 3:3 He will be like a refiner and purifier of silver; He will purify the sons of Levi and refine them like gold and silver. Then they will present offerings to the LORD in righteousness.

Refuge. Isaiah 25:4 For You have been a stronghold for the poor, a stronghold for the needy person in his distress, a refuge from the rain, a shade from the heat. When the breath of the violent is like rain against a wall,

Righteousness. 1 Corinthians 1:30 But it is from Him that you are in Christ Jesus, who became God-given wisdom for us — our righteousness, sanctification, and redemption,

Rock. Deuteronomy 32:15 hen Jeshurun became fat and rebelled - you became fat, bloated, and gorged. He abandoned the God who made him and scorned the Rock of his salvation.

Rod. Isaiah 11:1 Then a shoot (rod) will grow from the stump of Jesse, and a branch from his roots will bear fruit.

Rose of Sharon. Song of Songs 2:1 I am a rose of Sharon, a lily of the valleys.

Savior. Luke 2:11 Today a Savior, who is Messiah the Lord, was born for you in the city of David.

Seed of Abraham. Galatians 3:16 Now the promises were spoken to Abraham and to his seed. He does not say "and to seeds," as though referring to many, but referring to one, and to your seed, who is Christ.

Seed of David. 2 Timothy 2:8 Keep your attention on Jesus Christ as risen from the dead and descended from David. This is according to my gospel.

Seed of the woman. Genesis 3:15 I will put hostility between you and the woman, and between your seed and her seed. He will strike your head, and you will strike his heel.

Servant. Isaiah 42:1 This is My Servant; I strengthen Him, this is My Chosen One; I delight in Him. I have put My Spirit on Him; He will bring justice to the nations.

Servant of the Father. Matthew 12:18 Here is My Servant whom I have chosen, My beloved in whom My soul delights; I will put My Spirit on Him, and He will proclaim justice to the nations.

The Chief Shepherd. 1 Peter 5:4 And when the chief Shepherd appears, you will receive the unfading crown of glory.

The Good Shepherd. John 10:11 I am the good shepherd. The good shepherd lays down his life for the sheep.

The Great Shepherd. Hebrews 13:20 Now may the God of peace, who brought up from the dead our Lord Jesus — the great Shepherd of the sheep — with the blood of the everlasting covenant,

Shiloh. Genesis 49:10 The scepter will not depart from Judah or the staff from between his feet until He whose right it is comes and the obedience of the peoples belongs to Him.

Son of David. Matthew 9:27 As Jesus went on from there, two blind men followed Him, shouting, "Have mercy on us, Son of David!"

Son of Man. Mark 10:33 Listen! We are going up to Jerusalem. The Son of Man will be handed over to the chief priests and the scribes, and they will condemn Him to death. Then they will hand Him over to the Gentiles,

Son of God. Luke 1:35 ... Therefore, the holy One to be born will be called the Son of God.

Son of the Most High. Mark 5:7 And he cried out with a loud voice, "What do You have to do with me, Jesus, Son of the Most High God? I beg You before God, don't torment me!"

Son of Mary. Mark 6:3 Isn't this the carpenter, the son of Mary, and the brother of James, Joses, Judas, and Simon? And aren't His sisters here with us?" So they were offended by Him.

Son of The Most High. Luke 1:32 He will be great and will be called the Son of the Most High, and the Lord God will give Him the throne of His father David.

Stone. Matthew 21:42 The stone that the builders rejected has become the cornerstone. This came from the Lord and is wonderful in our eyes?

Sun of Righteousness. Malachi 4:2 But for you who fear My name, the sun of righteousness will rise with healing in its wings, and you will go out and playfully jump like calves from the stall.

Teacher. John 3:2 This man came to Him at night and said, " Rabbi, we know that You have come from God as a teacher, for no one could perform these signs You do unless God were with him."

The Amen. Revelation 3:14 "The Amen, the faithful and true Witness, the Originator of God's creation says:

The Highest. Luke 1:76 And child, you will be called a prophet of the Most High, for you will go before the Lord to prepare His ways,

The Just. 1 Peter 3:18 For Christ also suffered for sins once for all, the righteous for the unrighteous, that He might bring you to God, after being put to death in the fleshly realm but made alive in the spiritual realm.

The Mercy Seat or Propitiation for our sins. Romans 3:25 God presented Him as a propitiation through faith in His blood, to demonstrate His righteousness, because in His restraint God passed over the sins previously committed.

The Resurrection and the Life. John 11:25 "I am the resurrection and the life. The one who believes in Me, even if he dies, will live.

The Sacrifice. 1 John 4:10 Love consists in this: not that we loved God, but that He loved us and sent His Son to be the propitiation for our sins.

The Word. John 1:1 In the beginning was the Word, and the Word was with God, and the Word was God.

Tree of Life. Revelation 2:7 Anyone who has an ear should listen to what the Spirit says to the churches. I will give the victor the right to eat from the tree of life, which is in God's paradise.

True Bread from Heaven. John 16:32 Look: An hour is coming, and has come, when each of you will be scattered to his own home, and you will leave Me alone. Yet I am not alone, because the Father is with Me.

Who Was, and Is, and Is to Come. Revelation 4:8 Each of the four living creatures had six wings; they were covered with eyes around and inside. Day and night they never stop, saying: Holy, holy, holy, Lord God, the Almighty, who was, who is, and who is coming.

Wisdom of God. 1 Corinthians 1:24 Yet to those who are called, both Jews and Greeks, Christ is God's power and God's wisdom,

Wonderful. Isaiah 9:6 For a child will be born for us, a son will be given to us, and the government will be on His shoulders. He will be named Wonderful Counselor, Mighty God, Eternal Father, Prince of Peace.

Word of God. Revelation 19:13 He wore a robe stained with blood, and His name is the Word of God.

The Humanity Of Jesus Christ

Jesus Christ, in His profound humanity, was born of human parentage, possessing a body, soul, and spirit—a being wrapped in flesh and blood. He navigated the phases of life, maturing into adulthood, growing mentally, pondering and questioning. He embraced the essence of prayer, battled temptation, and learned obedience through lived experiences. His human form hungered, thirsted, wearied, and sought rest in sleep. Within His humanity, He exhibited the full spectrum of emotions—love and compassion, anger, grief, weeping, expressions of joy, and moments of deep trouble. His humanity reached its pinnacle when He sweat drops of blood, endured suffering, bled, and faced the finality of death, ultimately being buried. In His humanness, Jesus experienced the breadth of existence, embodying the very essence of human life while retaining divinity, an enigmatic blend that echoed the depth of His sacrifice for humanity.

Scriptures Concerning The Humanity Of Jesus Christ:

He had human parentage. Luke 1:31 You will conceive and give birth to a son, and you will call His name Jesus.

He had a body. Matthew 26:12 By pouring this fragrant oil on My body, she has prepared Me for burial.

He had a soul. John 12:27 Now My soul is troubled. What should I say — Father, save Me from this hour? But that is why I came to this hour.

He had a spirit. Mark 2:8 Right away Jesus understood in His spirit that they were thinking like this within themselves and said to them, "Why are you thinking these things in your hearts?

He had flesh and blood. Hebrews 2:14 Now since the children have flesh and blood in common, Jesus also shared in these, so that through His death He might destroy the one holding the power of death — that is, the Devil

He developed mentally and asked questions. Luke 2:46 After three days, they found Him in the temple complex sitting among the teachers, listening to them and asking them questions.

He prayed. Mark 1:35 Very early in the morning, while it was still dark, He got up, went out, and made His way to a deserted place. And He was praying there.

He was tempted. Matthew 4:1 Then Jesus was led up by the Spirit into the wilderness to be tempted by the Devil.

He learned obedience. Hebrews 5:8 Though He was God's Son, He learned obedience through what He suffered.

He hungered. Matthew 4:2 After He had fasted 40 days and 40 nights, He was hungry.

He thirsted. John 4:7 A woman of Samaria came to draw water. "Give Me a drink," Jesus said to her,

He grew tired. John 4:6 Jacob's well was there, and Jesus, worn out from His journey, sat down at the well. It was about six in the evening.

He slept. Matthew 8:24 Suddenly, a violent storm arose on the sea, so that the boat was being swamped by the waves. But He was sleeping.

He loved. Mark 10:21 Then, looking at him, Jesus loved him and said to him, "You lack one thing: Go, sell all you have and give to the poor, and you will have treasure in heaven. Then come, follow Me."

He had compassion. Matthew 9:36 When He saw the crowds, He felt compassion for them, because they were weary and worn out, like sheep without a shepherd.

He got angry and he grieved. Mark 3:5 After looking around at them with anger and sorrow at the hardness of their hearts, He told the man, "Stretch out your hand." So he stretched it out, and his hand was restored.

He wept. John 11:35 Jesus wept.

He expressed joy. Hebrews 12:2 keeping our eyes on Jesus, the source and perfecter of our faith, who for the joy that lay before Him endured a cross and despised the shame and has sat down at the right hand of God's throne.

He got troubled. John 11:33 When Jesus saw her crying, and the Jews who had come with her crying, He was angry in His spirit and deeply moved.

He sweat drops of blood. Luke 22:44 Being in anguish, He prayed more fervently, and His sweat became like drops of blood falling to the ground.

He suffered. 1 Peter 4:1 Therefore, since Christ suffered in the flesh, equip yourselves also with the same resolve — because the one who suffered in the flesh has finished with sin

He bled. John 19:34 But one of the soldiers pierced His side with a spear, and at once blood and water came out.

He died. Matthew 27:50 Jesus shouted again with a loud voice and gave up His spirit.

He was buried. Matthew 27:59 So Joseph took the body, wrapped it in clean, fine linen,

The Deity Of Jesus Christ

Jesus Christ is the second person of the Trinity, who embodies a divine nature fused seamlessly into a human body. He stands as 100% the Son of God and 100% the Son of Man. His omnipresence spans across time and space, while His omniscience comprehends all. As omnipotent, He reigns over disease, demons, humanity, nature, sin, traditions, and even death itself. His authority eclipses earthly limitations, showcasing unparalleled power that governs every aspect of existence, heralding a deity unmatched and unrivaled—an awe-inspiring testament to His divine essence and Sovereignty over all creation.

Jesus Christ is omnipresent. Matthew 18:20 For where two or three are gathered together in My name, I am there among them."

Jesus Christ is omniscient. John 2:24 Jesus, however, would not entrust Himself to them, since He knew them all.

Jesus Christ is omnipotent. Matthew 28:18 Then Jesus came near and said to them, "All authority has been given to Me in heaven and on earth.

Jesus Christ is omnipotent over disease. Matthew 8:1-4 When He came down from the mountain, large crowds followed Him. Right away a man with a serious skin disease came up and knelt before Him, saying, "Lord, if You are willing, You can make me clean." Reaching out His hand He touched him, saying, "I am willing; be made clean." Immediately his disease was healed. Then Jess told him, "See that you don't tell anyone; but go, show yourself to the priest, and offer the gift that Moses prescribed, as a testimony to them."

Jesus Christ is omnipotent over demons. Matthew 8:16 When evening came, they brought to Him many who were demon-possessed. He drove out the spirits with a word and healed all who were sick,

Jesus Christ is omnipotent over men. Matthew 9:9 As Jesus went on from there, He saw a man named Matthew sitting at the tax office, and He said to him, "Follow Me!" So he got up and followed Him.

Jesus Christ is omnipotent over nature. Matthew 8:26 But He said to them, "Why are you fearful, you of little faith?" Then He got up and rebuked the winds and the sea. And there was a great calm.

Jesus Christ is omnipotent over sin. Matthew 9:1-8 So He got into a boat, crossed over, and came to His own town. Just then some men brought to Him a paralytic lying on a mat. Seeing their faith, Jesus told the paralytic, "Have courage, son, your sins are forgiven." At this, some of the scribes said among themselves, "He's blaspheming!" But perceiving their thoughts, Jesus said, "Why are you thinking evil things in your hearts? For which is easier: to say, 'Your sins are forgiven,' or to say, 'Get up and walk'? But so you may know that the Son of Man has authority on earth to forgive sins" — then He told the paralytic, "Get up, pick up your mat, and go home." And he got up and went home. When the crowds saw this, they were awestruck and gave glory to God who had given such authority to men.

Jesus Christ is omnipotent over traditions. Matthew 9:10-17 While He was reclining at the table in the house, many tax collectors and sinners came as guests to eat with Jesus and His disciples. When the Pharisees saw this, they asked His disciples, "Why does your Teacher eat with tax collectors and sinners?" But when He heard this, He said, "Those who are well don't need a doctor, but the sick do. Go and learn what this means: I desire mercy and not sacrifice. For I didn't come to call the righteous, but sinners." Then John's disciples came to Him, saying, "Why do we and the Pharisees fast often, but

Your disciples do not fast?" Jesus said to them, "Can the wedding guests be sad while the groom is with them? The time will come when the groom will be taken away from them, and then they will fast. No one patches an old garment with unshrunk cloth, because the patch pulls away from the garment and makes the tear worse. And no one puts new wine into old wineskins. Otherwise, the skins burst, the wine spills out, and the skins are ruined. But they put new wine into fresh wineskins, and both are preserved."

Jesus Christ is omnipotent over death. Luke 7:14 Then He came up and touched the open coffin, and the pallbearers stopped. And He said, "Young man, I tell you, get up!"

The Sinlessness Of Christ.

When Christ took on flesh through the Body of Jesus, He took on sinless flesh, as sin is carried through the bloodline and can only be conquered through the bloodline.

Christ achieved what the adherents of the law could not do because the adherents of the law caried sin in their body and through the default of sin in the flesh ruling, all mankind fell.

Jesus who was without sin, condemned the sin that tried to rule in his body. Jesus not only conquered external temptations but conquered sin from the fallen nature inherited through Mary.

Hebrews 4:15 For we do not have a high priest who is unable to sympathize with our weaknesses, but One who has been tested in every way as we are, yet without sin.

James 1:14 But each person is tempted when he is drawn away and enticed by his own evil desires.

James 1:14 underscores Christ's monumental victory over temptation, enhancing His ability to understand and minister to our struggles with sin.

1 Corinthians 15:22, 45 "For just as in Adam all die, so also in Christ all will be made alive." "So also it is written, 'The first man, Adam, became a living person'; the last Adam became a life-giving spirit."

Being the last Adam implies that Christ came like Adam did and was without a sinful nature.

Where Adam fell when tempted by Satan, Christ did not.

Adam led his offspring into sin and death; while Christ led his offspring into righteousness and eternal life, and through faith in Christ, sin is removed and we now can have victory over all temptation and in holiness before God.

He knew no sin. 2 Corinthians 5:21 He made the One who did not know sin to be sin for us, so that we might become the righteousness of God in Him.

He did no sin. 1 Peter 2:22 He did not commit sin, and no deceit was found in His mouth;

He had no sin. 1 John 3:5 You know that He was revealed so that He might take away sins, and there is no sin in Him.

People Who Attested To Christ Being Sinless Were:

Pilate. John 19:4 Pilate went outside again and said to them, "Look, I'm bringing Him outside to you to let you know I find no grounds for charging Him."

Pilates wife. Matthew 27:19 While he was sitting on the judge's bench, his wife sent word to him, "Have nothing to do with that righteous man, for today I've suffered terribly in a dream because of Him!"

Judas. Matthew 27:4 "I have sinned by betraying innocent blood," he said. "What's that to us?" they said. "See to it yourself!"

The dying thief. Luke 23:41 We are punished justly, because we're getting back what we deserve for the things we did, but this man has done nothing wrong."

The Roman Centurion. Luke 23:47 When the centurion saw what happened, he began to glorify God, saying, "This man really was righteous!"

The Earthly Ministry Of Jesus Christ.

The recorded ministry of Jesus Christ started at the age of 12 years old when Jesus Christ was asking questions to the Priests in the temple, and culminated in His ascension into Heaven.

The ministry of Jesus Christ has been and still is being, made manifest through the body of Jesus Christ called the Church. As members of the Body of Jesus Christ, we the Church exercise His authority through the Kingdom of God's expansion to the ends of the earth.

Jesus at the age of 12 years old. Luke 2:42 When He was 12 years old, they went up according to the custom of the festival.

Jesus at His baptism. Matthew 3:16 After Jesus was baptized, He went up immediately from the water. The heavens suddenly opened for Him, and He saw the Spirit of God descending like a dove and coming down on Him.

Jesus chose the twelve. Matthew 10:1 Summoning His 12 disciples, He gave them authority over unclean spirits, to drive them out and to heal every disease and sickness.

Jesus at His temptation. Matthew 4:1 Then Jesus was led up by the Spirit into the wilderness to be tempted by the Devil.

Jesus at His first miracle in Cana. John 2:11 Jesus performed this first sign in Cana of Galilee. He displayed His glory, and His disciples believed in Him.

Jesus cleansing the temple. John 2:16 "Get these things out of here! Stop turning My Father's house into a marketplace!"

Jesus and His sermon on Isaiah. Luke 4:17 The scroll of the prophet Isaiah was given to Him, and unrolling the scroll, He found the place where it was written:

Jesus and the parable of the Sower. Matthew 13:19 When anyone hears the word about the kingdom and doesn't understand it, the evil one comes and snatches away what was sown in his heart. This is the one sown along the path.

Jesus feeding the 5000. John 6:10,11 Then Jesus said, "Have the people sit down." There was plenty of grass in that place, so they sat down. The men numbered about 5,000. Then Jesus took the loaves, and after giving thanks

He distributed them to those who were seated — so also with the fish, as much as they wanted.

Jesus walking on the water. John 6:19 ... they saw Jesus walking on the sea. He was coming near the boat, and they were afraid.

Jesus forgives the adulterous woman. John 8:4 "Teacher," they said to Him, "this woman was caught in the act of committing adultery.

Jesus healing a blind man. John 8:22-24 They brought a blind man to Him and begged Him to touch him. He took the blind man by the hand and brought him out of the village. Spitting on his eyes and laying His hands on him, He asked him, "Do you see anything?" He looked up and said, "I see people — they look to me like trees walking."

Jesus and the sermon of the Good Shepherd. John 10:14,15 I am the good shepherd. I know My own sheep, and they know Me, as the Father knows Me, and I know the Father.

Jesus, Moses and Elijah, with Peter James and John on the transfiguration. Matthew 17:2 He was transformed in front of them, and His face shone like the sun. Even His clothes became as white as the light.

Anointing from Mary of Bethany. John 12:4 Then Mary took a pound of fragrant oil — pure and expensive nard — anointed Jesus' feet, and wiped His feet with her hair. So the house was filled with the fragrance of the oil.

His triumphal entry. Mt. 21:10 When He entered Jerusalem, the whole city was shaken, saying, "Who is this?"

The Last Supper. John 13:2 Now by the time of supper, the Devil had already put it into the heart of Judas, Simon Iscariot's son, to betray Him

His arrest at Gethsemane. John 18:2 Judas, who betrayed Him, also knew the place, because Jesus often met there with His disciples.

The trial of condemnation by Pilot. John 19:1-16 Then Pilate took Jesus and had Him flogged. ...

The crucifixion. John 19:17-37 Carrying His own cross, He went out to what is called Skull Place, which in Hebrew is called Golgotha. ...

The conversion of the dying thief. Luke 23:34 "Father, forgive them, because they do not know what they are doing."

His glorious resurrection. Matthew 28:2-4 Suddenly there was a violent earthquake because an angel of the Lord descended from heaven and approached the tomb. He rolled back the stone and was sitting on it. His appearance was like lightning, and his robe was as white as snow. The guards were so shaken from fear of him that they became like dead men.

The appearance to Mary Magdalene. John 20:1-18 On the first day of the week Mary Magdalene came to the tomb early, while it was still dark. She saw that the stone had been removed from the tomb. ….

The appearance on the Emmaus Road. Luke 24:15 while they were discussing and arguing, Jesus Himself came near and began to walk along with them.

The appearance to his disciples. Luke 24:38,39 "Why are you troubled?" He asked them. "And why do doubts arise in your hearts? Look at My hands and My feet, that it is I Myself! Touch Me and see, because a ghost does not have flesh and bones as you can see I have."

His ascension into heaven. Luke 24:51 And while He was blessing them, He left them and was carried up into heaven.

The Character Of Jesus.

The character of Jesus Christ resonated through His actions and words revealing His fervent zeal and commitment to the house of God, with a consuming fire within Him, igniting an urgency for transformation. His compassion knew no bounds, extending to the multitudes, the sick, the hungry, the widowed, the leprous, the afflicted father, and the demonized, weaving a tapestry of empathy that enveloped all in need. His meekness and gentleness were evidenced in His tender care for human infirmities and the humble act of washing His disciples' feet, revealing the depth of His servitude. Courage radiated from His being, fearlessly confronting historical unbelief, and religion, cleansing the temple, ministering to the tormented, resurrecting Lazarus, confronting the Pharisees' wickedness, and enduring the agonizing path to Calvary. Love was His cornerstone, emanating towards His Father with unwavering devotion, embracing His disciples, cherishing little children, displaying profound affection for select friends, and enveloping the city of Jerusalem in a love transcending time and circumstance.

In Jesus' multifaceted character, we see the zeal, compassion, meekness, courage, and boundless love, leaving an unparalleled impartation that continues to inspire and impart to all who believe in Him.

Here are some of His characteristics to consider.

His zeal for Israel and the Church. John 2:17 Zeal for Your House has consumed Me.

His compassion towards the multitudes. Matthew 9:36 When He saw the crowds, He felt compassion for them, because they were weary and worn out, like sheep without a shepherd.

His compassion towards the sick. Matthew 14:14 As He stepped ashore, He saw a huge crowd, felt compassion for them, and healed their sick.

His compassion towards the hungry. Matthew 15:32 "I have compassion on the crowd, because they've already stayed with Me three days and have nothing to eat. I don't want to send them away hungry; otherwise, they might collapse on the way."

His compassion towards the widow. Luke 7:13 When the Lord saw her, He had compassion on her and said, "Don't cry."

His compassion towards the lepper. Mark 1: 41 Moved with compassion, Jesus reached out His hand and touched him. "I am willing," He told him. "Be made clean."

His compassion towards the father. Mark 9:22 "And many times it has thrown him into fire or water to destroy him. But if You can do anything, have compassion on us and help us."

His compassion towards the demonized person. Mark 5:19 But He would not let him; instead, He told him, "Go back home to your own people, and report to them how much the Lord has done for you and how He has had mercy on you."

His meekness and gentleness in dealing with our infirmities. Matthew 12:18-21 Here is My Servant whom I have chosen, My beloved in whom My soul delights; I will put My Spirit on Him, and He will proclaim justice to the nations. He will not argue or shout, and no one will hear His voice in the streets. He will not break a bruised reed, and He will not put out a smoldering wick until He has led justice to victory. The nations will put their hope in His name.

His meekness and gentleness in washing the feet of his disciples. John 13:4,5 So He got up from supper, laid aside His robe, took a towel, and tied it around Himself. Next, He poured water into a basin and began to wash His disciples' feet and to dry them with the towel tied around Him.

His meekness and gentleness through his own words. Matthew 11:28-30 Come to Me, all of you who are weary and burdened, and I will give you rest. All of you, take up My yoke and learn from Me, because I am gentle and humble in heart, and you will find rest for yourselves. For My yoke is easy and My burden is light.

His meekness and gentleness in the suffering and death. Isaiah 53:7 He was oppressed and afflicted, yet He did not open His mouth. Like a lamb led to the slaughter and like a sheep silent before her shearers, He did not open His mouth.

His courage in cleaning the temple. John 2:14-17 In the temple complex He found people selling oxen, sheep, and doves, and He also found the money changers sitting there. After making a whip out of cords, He drove everyone out of the temple complex with their sheep and oxen. He also poured out the money changers' coins and overturned the tables. He told those who were selling doves, "Get these things out of here! Stop turning My Father's house into a marketplace!"

And His disciples remembered that it is written: Zeal for Your house will consume Me.

His courage when he ministered fearlessly to a madman. Mark 5:2-8 As soon as He got out of the boat, a man with an unclean spirit came out of the tombs and met Him. He lived in the tombs. No one was able to restrain him anymore — even with chains — because he often had been bound with shackles and chains, but had snapped off the chains and smashed the shackles. No one was strong enough to subdue him. And always, night and day, he was crying out among the tombs and in the mountains and cutting himself with stones. When he saw Jesus from a distance, he ran and knelt down before Him. And he cried out with a loud voice, "What do You have to do with me, Jesus, Son of the Most High God? I beg You before God, don't torment me!" For He had told him, "Come out of the man, you unclean spirit!"

His courage when He raised Lazarus from the dead. John 11:6-8 So when He heard that he was sick, He stayed two more days in the place where He was. Then after that, He said to the disciples, "Let's go to Judea again." " Rabbi," the disciples told Him, "just now the Jews tried to stone You, and You're going there again?"

His courage when he denounced the wickedness of the Pharisees. Matthew 23:13 But woe to you, scribes and Pharisees, hypocrites! You lock up the kingdom of heaven from people. For you don't go in, and you don't allow those entering to go in.

His courage when he walked to Calvary. Mark 10:32-34 But woe to you, scribes and Pharisees, hypocrites! You lock up the kingdom of heaven from people. For you don't go in, and you don't allow those entering to go in.

His love towards his father. John 14:31 I am going away so that the world may know that I love the Father.

His love towards his disciples. John 13:34 I give you a new command: Love one another. Just as I have loved you, you must also love one another.

His love towards little children. Mark 10:13-16 Some people were bringing little children to Him so He might touch them, but His disciples rebuked them. When Jesus saw it, He was indignant and said to them, "Let the little children come to Me. Don't stop them, for the kingdom of God belongs to such as these. I assure you: Whoever does not welcome the kingdom of God like a little child will never enter it." After taking them in His arms, He laid His hands on them and blessed them.

His love towards certain close friends. John 11:1-3 So the sisters sent a message to Him: "Lord, the one You love is sick."

His love towards the city of Jerusalem. Matthew 23:37 Jerusalem, Jerusalem! She who kills the prophets and stones those who are sent to her. How often I wanted to gather your children together, as a hen gathers her chicks under her wings, yet you were not willing!

The Kenosis Of Christ.

The term kenosis refers to the doctrine of Christ's "self-emptying" in His incarnation. The word comes from the Greek of Philippians 2:7 Instead He emptied Himself by assuming the form of a slave, taking on the likeness of men. And when He had come as a man in His external form.

The word emptied in Greek is kenosis and means that Christ took on the a human nature with all its limitations, except with no sin.
Christ's emptying of Himself was the laying aside of the Divine Heavenly privileges that were His, and rather than stay on His throne in heaven, Jesus

"made himself of no repute and lowered himself to the level of fallen mankind.

The kenosis experience was a self-renunciation and in no ways an emptying of His deity. Nor was it an exchange of deity for humanity. Jesus never ceased to be God during any part of His earthly ministry. He did set aside His heavenly glory. He also voluntarily refrained from using His divinity to make His way easier. During His earthly ministry, Christ completely submitted Himself to the will of the Father

Christ who is the Son of God never performed a miracle or used any of Divine Deity to perform the miraculous while walking on the earth in the body of Jesus.

Philippians 2:5-11   Have this mind in you, which was also in Christ Jesus: who, existing in the form of God, counted not the being on an equality with God a thing to be grasped, but emptied himself, taking the form of a servant, being made in the likeness of men; and being found in fashion as a man, he humbled himself, becoming obedient even unto death, yea, the death of the cross. Wherefore also God highly exalted him, and gave unto him the name which is above every name; that in the name of Jesus every knee should bow, of things in heaven and things on earth and things under the earth, and that every tongue should confess that Jesus Christ is Lord, to the glory of God the Father.

The above scripture implies that Christ left His home in Glory, and made himself of no reputation. He abstained from his omnipresence for a period.

He abstained from his omniscience for a period. Mark 13:32 Now concerning that day or hour no one knows — neither the angels in heaven nor the Son — except the Father.

He Abstained from his omnipotence for a period. John 4:19,20 Sir," the woman replied, "I see that You are a prophet. Our fathers worshiped on this mountain, yet you Jews say that the place to worship is in Jerusalem.

He was made in the likeness of man. John 1:14 The Word became flesh and took up residence among us. We observed His glory, the glory as the One and Only Son from the Father, full of grace and truth.

He humbled himself. 1 Peter 2:21-24 For you were called to this,
because Christ also suffered for you, leaving you an example, so that you should follow in His steps. He did not commit sin, and no deceit was found in His mouth; when He was reviled, He did not revile in return; when He was suffering, He did not threaten but entrusted Himself to the One who judges justly. He Himself bore our sins in His body on the tree, so that, having died to sins, we might live for righteousness; you have been healed by His wounds.

He became obedient unto death. Philippians 2:8 He humbled Himself by becoming obedient to the point of death — even to death on a cross.

He has been highly exalted by the Father and given a name that is above all names. Philippians 2:9 For this reason God highly exalted Him and gave Him the name that is above every name,

The Resurrection And Proof Of His Appearances.

There is no other single doctrine in the Bible that the devil hates as much as the truth and doctrine of the resurrection of Christ.
The devil has always attempted to discredit the resurrection of Jesus Christ, yet he has been unsuccessful in his attempts to downplay, deny, discredit or simply plan it away.

There are many proven facts with evidence of Jesus Christ's resurrection, some of them are below.

The empty tomb. Luke 24:2,3 They found the stone rolled away from the tomb. They went in but did not find the body of the Lord Jesus.

The nail scared hands of Jesus. John 20:27 Put your finger here and observe My hands. Reach out your hand and put it into My side. Don't be an unbeliever, but a believer.

The Romans guarding the tomb of Jesus. Matthew 27:65 You have a guard of soldiers," Pilate told them. "Go and make it as secure as you know how."

To Mary Magdalene. John 20: 16 Jesus said, "Mary." Turning around, she said to Him in Hebrew, "Rabbouni!" — which means "Teacher."

To other women who were returning to the tomb. Matthew 28; 9-10 Just then Jesus met them and said, "Good morning!" They came up, took hold of His feet, and worshiped Him. Then Jesus told them, "Do not be afraid. Go and tell My brothers to leave for Galilee, and they will see Me there."

To (Simon) Peter in the afternoon. Luke 24:34 "The Lord has certainly been raised, and has appeared to Simon!"

To the disciples on the road to Emmaus. Mark 16:12,13 Then after this, He appeared in a different form to two of them walking on their way into the country. And they went and reported it to the rest, who did not believe them either.

To the 10 disciples, Thomas was not there. Mark 16:14 Later, He appeared to the Eleven themselves as they were reclining at the table. He rebuked their unbelief and hardness of heart, because they did not believe those who saw Him after He had been resurrected.

To the 11 disciples a week later. John 20:26-29 After eight days His disciples were indoors again, and Thomas was with them. Even though the doors were locked, Jesus came and stood among them. He said, "Peace to you!" Then He said to Thomas, "Put your finger here and observe My hands. Reach out your hand and put it into My side. Don't be an unbeliever, but a believer." Thomas responded to Him, "My Lord and my God!" Jesus said, "Because you have seen Me, you have believed. Those who believe without seeing are blessed."

To 7 disciples by the sea of Galilee. John 21:1-23 After this, Jesus revealed Himself again to His disciples by the Sea of Tiberias. He revealed Himself in this way: ...

To the 500. 1 Corinthians 15:6 Then He appeared to over 500 brothers at one time; most of them are still alive, but some have fallen asleep.

To James the brother of Jesus. 1 Corinthians 15:7 Then He appeared to James, then to all the apostles.

To the writer of the book of Corinthians. 1 Corinthians 15:8 Last of all, as to one abnormally born, He also appeared to me.

To the 11 disciples on the mountain in Galilee. Matthew 28:16-20 The 11 disciples traveled to Galilee, to the mountain where Jesus had directed them. When they saw Him, they worshiped, but some doubted. Then Jesus came near and said to them, "All authority has been given to Me in heaven and on earth. Go, therefore, and make disciples of all nations, baptizing them in the name of the Father and of the Son and of the Holy Spirit, teaching them to observe everything I have commanded you. And remember, I am with you always, to the end of the age."

To the 11 disciples at his ascension from the Mount of Olives. Luke 24:50,51 Then He led them out as far as Bethany, and lifting up His hands He blessed them. And while He was blessing them, He left them and was carried up into heaven.

To Stephen just before he was martyred. Acts 7:55,56 But Stephen, filled by the Holy Spirit, gazed into heaven. He saw God's glory, with Jesus standing at the right hand of God, and he said, "Look! I see the heavens opened and the Son of Man standing at the right hand of God!"

To Saul on the road to Damascus. Acts 9:4,5 "Saul, Saul, why are you persecuting Me?" "Who are You, Lord?" he said. "I am Jesus, the One you are persecuting,"

To Paul in Arabia. Acts 26:15 Then I said, 'Who are You, Lord?'
"And the Lord replied: 'I am Jesus, the One you are persecuting.

To Paul in the temple when Paul was warned concerning the persecution which was to come. Acts 22:17 After I came back to Jerusalem and was praying in the temple complex, I went into a visionary state and saw Him telling me, 'Hurry and get out of Jerusalem quickly because they will not accept your testimony about Me!'

To Paul while he was in prison in Caesarea. Acts 23:11 The following night, the Lord stood by him and said, "Have courage! For as you have testified about Me in Jerusalem, so you must also testify in Rome."

To the apostle John on the isle of Patmos while receiving his Revelation. Revelation 1:12-20 I turned to see whose voice it was that spoke to me. When I turned I saw seven gold lampstands, and among the lampstands was One like the Son of Man, dressed in a long robe and with a gold sash wrapped around His chest. His head and hair were white like wool — white as snow — and His eyes like a fiery flame. His feet were like fine bronze as it is fired in a furnace, and His voice like the sound of cascading waters. He had seven stars in His right hand; a sharp double-edged sword came from His mouth, and His face was shining like the sun at midday. When I saw Him, I fell at His feet like a dead man. He laid His right hand on me and said, "Don't be afraid! I am the First and the Last, and the Living One. I was dead, but look — I am alive forever and ever, and I hold the keys of death and Hades. Therefore write what you have seen, what is, and what will take place after this. The secret of the seven stars you saw in My right hand and of the seven gold lampstands is this: The seven stars are the angels of the seven churches, and the seven lampstands are the seven churches.

BIBLE DOCTRINE

Present-Day Ministry Of Jesus Christ

He sits at Father's right hand and at the same time is kneeling before the Father with purpose to be:

Je is your forerunner. Hebrews 6:19,20 We have this hope as an anchor for our lives, safe and secure. It enters the inner sanctuary behind the curtain. Jesus has entered there on our behalf as a forerunner because He has become a high priest forever in the order of Melchizedek.

He is praying for you. Hebrews 7:25 He always lives to make intercession for them."

He has gone to prepare a place for us. John 14:2 In My Father's house are many dwelling places; if not, I would have told you. I am going away to prepare a place for you.

He has given spiritual gifts to His followers. Ephesians 4:11,12 And He personally gave some to be apostles, some prophets, some evangelists, some pastors, and teachers, for the training of the saints in the work of ministry, to build up the body of Christ,

Offer encouragement to His followers. Hebrews 4:14-16 Therefore, since we have a great high priest who has passed through the heavens — Jesus the Son of God — let us hold fast to the confession. For we do not have a high priest who is unable to sympathize with our weaknesses, but One who has been tested in every way as we are, yet without sin. Therefore let us approach the throne of grace with boldness, so that we may receive mercy and find grace to help us at the proper time.

Make high priestly prayers for us. Romans 8:34 Who is the one who condemns? Christ Jesus is the One who died, but even more, has been raised; He also is at the right hand of God and intercedes for us.

Send the promise of the Father. Acts 2:33 Therefore, since He has been exalted to the right hand of God and has received from the Father the promised Holy Spirit, He has poured out what you both see and hear.

Care for His Church. Revelation 3:22 "Anyone who has an ear should listen to what the Spirit says to the churches."

Work through His people. John 14:12 You aren't greater than our father Jacob, are You? He gave us the well and drank from it himself, as did his sons and livestock."

Wait until His enemies become His footstool. Hebrews 10:13 He is now waiting until His enemies are made His footstool.

Return of Jesus Christ.

A few hours before the birth of Jesus, Mary rode on a donkey into Bethlehem.

When Jesus returns for the second time, He will be mounted on a white horse.

His arrival in Bethlehem as a baby fulfilled prophecy and fulfilled many messianic predictions throughout His life, ministry, death, and resurrection. Nonetheless, certain prophetic words about the Messiah remain unaccomplished. His Second Coming will fulfill these prophecies, shifting from a suffering Servant to a victorious King. During His first coming, Jesus entered the world with utmost humility, shattering the expectations of Jewish leaders. However, upon His return, He will arrive accompanied by the heavenly armies, showcasing His divine Sovereignty, Supreme Authority, and All Power, emphasizing His reign as the conquering King foretold in scripture.

In the last Chapter of this Book, you will find the Doctrine of Eschatology and more on the subject of the second coming of Jesus Christ.

BIBLE DOCTRINE

DOCTRINE OF THE HOLY SPIRIT

The Holy Spirit is the third person of The Triune God, and is coequal and coeternal with the Father and the Son.

The Holy Spirit is the expressed power of the Trinity, and it is most important that He is not grieved or removes His presence, since there is no further appeal to the Father and Son on the day of redemption (Ephesians 4:30 And don't grieve God's Holy Spirit. You were sealed by Him for the day of redemption.).

The Holy Spirit manifests Himself as the Grace of God by which believers come to Christ through salvation, and thus He is closer to us than we are to ourselves.

Like the eyes of the body, which see in the natural, so is the Holy Spirit in revealing Father and Son to us.

The Holy Spirit is never referred to as a depersonalized force and is seldom the focus of attention.

The Holy Spirit is the One through whom all else is seen. This explains why the revelation of the Father and the Son in the Gospels is viewed more than that of The Holy Spirit Himself. It is because, through the inspiration and revelation from the Holy Spirit, we gain understanding and relationship with Father, Son, and Holy Spirit.

The Personality Of The Holy Spirit.

The SPIRIT of God is a person, as much as the FATHER and SON are a person.

The person of the Holy Spirit is confirmed by His workings throughout the Bible and is known as the Paraclete, or Helper, whom Jesus promised the Father would send.

The Holy Spirit reveals and unveils Himself and the deep mysteries of God to those who choose to be seekers of the Kingdom of God.

Below are some of the ways the Holy Spirit revealed His persona.

He has a mind. Romans 8:27 And He who searches the hearts knows the Spirit's mind-set, because He intercedes for the saints according to the will of God.

He searches out the human mind. 1 Corinthians 2:10 Now God has revealed these things to us by the Spirit, for the Spirit searches everything, even the depths of God. He searches all things.

He has a will works according to his own will. 1 Corinthians 12:11 But one and the same Spirit is active in all these, distributing to each person as He wills.

He has a power of his own. Romans 15:13 Now may the God of hope fill you with all joy and peace as you believe in Him so that you may overflow with hope by the power of the Holy Spirit.

He testifies of Christ. John 15;26 When the Counselor comes, the One I will send to you from the Father — the Spirit of truth who proceeds from the Father — He will testify about Me.

He glorifies Christ. John 16:14 He will glorify Me, because He will take from what is Mine and declare it to you.

He loves. John 14:21 The one who has My commands and keeps them is the one who loves Me. And the one who loves Me will be loved by My Father. I also will love him and will reveal Myself to him."

He teaches. John 14:26 But the Counselor, the Holy Spirit — the Father will send Him in My name — will teach you all things and remind you of everything I have told you.

He spoke through the David. Acts 1:16 Brothers, the Scripture had to be fulfilled that the Holy Spirit through the mouth of David spoke in advance about Judas, who became a guide to those who arrested Jesus.

He speaks.

>To Phillip in the desert. Acts 8:29 The Spirit told Philip, "Go and join that chariot."
>
>To Peter on the house top. Acts 10:19 While Peter was thinking about the vision, the Spirit told him, "Three men are here looking for you.
>
>To some elders in Antioch. Acts 13:2 As they were ministering to the Lord and fasting, the Holy Spirit said, "Set apart for Me Barnabas and Saul for the work I have called them to."
>
>To 7 churches in Asia minor to. Revelation 2-3 Write to the angel of the church in Ephesus: ...

He grieves. Ephesians 4:30 And don't grieve God's Holy Spirit. You were sealed by Him for the day of redemption.

He comforts. Acts 9:31 So the church throughout all Judea, Galilee, and Samaria had peace, being built up and walking in the fear of the Lord and in the encouragement of the Holy Spirit, and it increased in numbers.

He prays. Romans 8:26 In the same way the Spirit also joins to help in our weakness, because we do not know what to pray for as we should, but the Spirit Himself intercedes for us with unspoken groanings.

He creates and gives life. Job 33:4 And don't grieve God's Holy Spirit. You were sealed by Him for the day of redemption.

He sanctifies. Romans 15:16 to be a minister of Christ Jesus to the Gentiles, serving as a priest of God's good news. My purpose is that the offering of the Gentiles may be acceptable, sanctified by the Holy Spirit.

He dwells with saints. John 14:17 He is the Spirit of truth. The world is unable to receive Him because it doesn't see Him or know Him. But you do know Him, because He remains with you and will be in you.

He appoints and commissions ministers. Isaiah 48:16 Approach Me and listen to this. From the beginning I have not spoken in secret; from the time anything existed, I was there." And now the Lord GOD has sent me and His Spirit.

He guides. John 16:13 When the Spirit of truth comes, He will guide you into all the truth. For He will not speak on His own, but He will speak whatever He hears. He will also declare to you what is to come.

He directs ministers where to preach. Acts 8:29 The Spirit told Philip, "Go and join that chariot."

He directs ministers where not to preach. Acts 16:6 They went through the region of Phrygia and Galatia and were prevented by the Holy Spirit from speaking the message in Asia.

He instructs ministers on what to preach. 1 Corinthians 2:13 We also speak these things, not in words taught by human wisdom, but in those taught by the Spirit, explaining spiritual things to spiritual people.

He reproves. John 16:8 When He comes, He will convict the world about sin, righteousness, and judgment:

He forbids. Acts 16:6,7 They went through the region of Phrygia and Galatia and were prevented by the Holy Spirit from speaking the message in Asia. When they came to Mysia, they tried to go into Bithynia, but the Spirit of Jesus did not allow them.

He strives with sinners. Genesis 6:3 And the LORD said, "My Spirit will not remain with mankind forever, because they are corrupt. Their days will be 120 years."

He permits. Acts 16:10 After he had seen the vision, we immediately made efforts to set out for Macedonia, concluding that God had called us to evangelize them.

He can be vexed. Isaiah 63:10 But they rebelled and grieved His Holy Spirit. So, He became their enemy and fought against them.

He can be resisted. Acts 7:51 You stiff-necked people with uncircumcised hearts and ears! You are always resisting the Holy Spirit; as your ancestors did, so do you.

He can be tempted. Acts 5:9 Then Peter said to her, "Why did you agree to test the Spirit of the Lord? Look! The feet of those who have buried your husband are at the door, and they will carry you out!"

The Deity Of The Holy Spirit.

The Holy Spirit is the third person of the Trinity. Isaiah 9:6

There are 4 distinct proofs of the deity of the Holy Spirit.

1. Omnipotence. Luke 1:35 The Holy Spirit will come upon you, Therefore, the holy One to be born will be called the Son of God and the power of the Most High will overshadow you.
2. Omniscience. 1 Corinthians 2:10-11 Now God has revealed these things to us by the Spirit, for the Spirit searches everything, even the depths of God. For who among men knows the thoughts of a man except the spirit of the man that is in him? In the same way, no one knows the thoughts of God except the Spirit of God.
3. Omnipresence. Psalms 139:7 Where can I go to escape Your Spirit? Where can I flee from Your presence?
4. Eternal. Hebrews 9:14 how much more will the blood of the Messiah, who through the eternal Spirit offered Himself without blemish to God, cleanse our consciences from dead works to serve the living God?

The Names And Titles Of The Holy Spirit.

Spirit of YHWH God. Acts 5:9 Then Peter said to her, "Why did you agree to test the Spirit of the Lord?

Breath of the Almighty. Job 33:4 The Spirit of God has made me, and the breath of the Almighty gives me life.

The Spirit of Comfort. John 14:16 And I will ask the Father, and He will give you another Counselor to be with you forever.

The Eternal Spirit. Hebrews 9:14 how much more will the blood of the Messiah, who through the Eternal Spirit offered Himself without blemish to God, cleanse our consciences from dead works to serve the living God?

The Spirit. Matthew 4:1 Then Jesus was led up by the Spirit into the wilderness to be tempted by the Devil.

The Holy Spirit. Psalms 51:11 Do not banish me from Your presence or take Your Holy Spirit from me.

Spirit of the Lord God. Isaiah 61:1 The Spirit of the Lord GOD is on Me,…

Spirit of God. Genesis 1:2 Now the earth was formless and empty, darkness covered the surface of the watery depths, and the Spirit of God was hovering over the surface of the waters.

Spirit of the Father. Matthew 10:20 because you are not speaking, but the Spirit of your Father is speaking through you.

Spirit of Christ. Romans 8:9 You, however, are not in the flesh, but in the Spirit, since the Spirit of God lives in you. But if anyone does not have the Spirit of Christ, he does not belong to Him.

Spirit of the Son. Galatians 4:6 And because you are sons, God has sent the Spirit of His Son into our hearts, crying, " Abba, Father!"

Spirit of life. Romans 8:2 because the Spirit's law of life in Christ Jesus has set you free from the law of sin and of death.

Spirit of grace. Zechariah 12:10 Then I will pour out a spirit of grace and prayer on the house of David and the residents of Jerusalem, and they will look at Me whom they pierced. They will mourn for Him as one mourns for an only child and weep bitterly for Him as one weeps for a firstborn.

Spirit of prophecy. Revelation 19:10 Then I fell at his feet to worship him, but he said to me, "Don't do that! I am a fellow slave with you and your brothers who have the testimony about Jesus. Worship God, because the testimony about Jesus is the spirit of prophecy."

Spirit of adoption. Romans 8:15 For you did not receive a spirit of slavery to fall back into fear, but you received the Spirit of adoption, by whom we cry out, " Abba, Father!"

Spirit of truth. John 14:17 He is the Spirit of truth. The world is unable to receive Him because it doesn't see Him or know Him. But you do know Him, because He remains with you and will be in you.

Spirit of holiness. Romans 1:4 and who has been declared to be the powerful Son of God by the resurrection from the dead according to the Spirit of holiness.

Spirit of revelation. Ephesians 1:17 I pray that the God of our Lord Jesus Christ, the glorious Father, would give you a spirit of wisdom and revelation in the knowledge of Him.

Spirit of judgment and Spirit of burning. Isaiah 4:4 when the Lord has washed away the filth of the daughters of Zion and cleansed the bloodguilt from the heart of Jerusalem by a spirit of judgment and a spirit of burning.

Spirit of glory. 1 Peter 4:14 If you are ridiculed for the name of Christ, you are blessed, because the Spirit of glory and of God rests on you.

Seven Spirits of God. Revelation 1:4 Grace and peace to you from the One who is, who was, and who is coming; from the seven spirits before His throne;

Free Spirit. Psalms 51:12 Restore the joy of Your salvation to me, and give me a willing spirit.

Good Spirit. Nehemiah 9:20 You sent Your good Spirit to instruct them. You did not withhold Your manna from their mouths, and You gave them water for their thirst.

The Lord. 2 Thessalonians. 3:5 May the Lord direct your hearts to God's love and Christ's endurance.

Power of the Highest. Luke 1:35 The angel replied to her: "The Holy Spirit will come upon you, and the power of the Most High will overshadow you. Therefore, the holy One to be born will be called the Son of God.

And in Isaiah 11:2 we see the Holy spirit reveal Himself as The Spirit of the LORD, The Spirit of wisdom and understanding, The Spirit of counsel and strength, The Spirit of knowledge, and of the fear of the LORD.

The Emblems Of The Holy Spirit.

The emblems and symbols of the Holy Spirit are invisible, glorious, awe-inspiring, and gentle, revealing the magnificence of His being.

The Holy Spirit never talks about Himself, His entire focus is to glorify the Father and glorify Jesus Christ.

The secondary focus of the Holy Spirit is to reveal the Father and Son to you in an objective way of imparting truth, and also in the subjective way that He comes to penetrate your life.

When we talk about the Holy Spirit as rain, the purpose isn't to think, "Oh, the Holy Spirit is like rain." The purpose is to get wet.

Just as the Holy Spirit manifested like a dove and lighted upon Jesus, so the Holy Spirit wants to penetrate you with the glory of the invisible God who becomes visible in you, so that you can radiate His Glory, bringing honor to the Father and being a witness to the world.

The Nine Emblems And Application Of The Holy Spirit.

1. The Holy Spirit is like Water. John 3:5 Jesus answered, "I assure you: Unless someone is born of water and the Spirit, he cannot enter the kingdom of God.
   - The washing of the Holy Spirit. Ezek. 16:9 I washed you with water, rinsed off your blood, and anointed you with oil.
   - The fertilization of the Holy Spirit. Psalms 1:3 He is like a tree planted beside streams of water that bears its fruit in season and whose leaf does not wither. Whatever he does prospers.
   - The refreshing of the Holy Spirit. Psalms 46:4 There is a river — its streams delight the city of God, the holy dwelling place of the Most High.
   - The abundance of the Holy Spirit. Joel 2:28 I will pour out My Spirit on all humanity;
   - The Holy Spirit is freely given. Is 55:1 Come, everyone who is thirsty, come to the waters; and you without money, come, buy, and eat! Come, buy wine and milk without money and without cost!

2. The Holy Spirit like fire. Matthew 3:11 I baptize you with water for repentance, but the One who is coming after me is more powerful than I. I am not worthy to remove His sandals. He Himself will baptize you with the Holy Spirit and fire.
   - Purifying fire of the Holy Spirit. Isaiah 4:4 when the Lord has washed away the filth of the daughters of Zion and cleansed the bloodguilt from the heart of Jerusalem by a spirit of judgment and a spirit of burning.
   - Illuminating fire of the Holy Spirit. Exodus 13:21 The LORD went ahead of them in a pillar of cloud to lead them on their way during the day and in a pillar of fire to give them light at night, so that they could travel day or night.
   - Searching fire of the Holy Spirit. Zeph 1:12 and at that time I will search Jerusalem with lamps and punish the men who settle down comfortably, who say to themselves: The LORD will not do good or evil.
3. The Holy Spirit like wind.

Independence of the Holy Spirit. John 3:8 The wind blows where it pleases, and you hear its sound, but you don't know where it comes from or where it is going. So it is with everyone born of the Spirit."
   - The power of the Holy Spirit. Luke 1:35 The angel answered and said to her, "The Holy Spirit will come upon you, and the power

of the Most High will overshadow you; and for that reason, the holy Child shall be called the Son of God.

- The reviving wind of the Holy Spirit. Ezekiel 37:9 He said to me, "Prophesy to the breath, prophesy, son of man. Say to it: This is what the Lord GOD says: Breath, come from the four winds and breathe into these slain so that they may live!"

4. The Holy Spirit is like oil. Psalms 45:7 You love righteousness and hate wickedness; therefore God, your God, has anointed you with the oil of joy more than your companions.

- The healing oil of the Holy Spirit. Luke 10:34 He went over to him and bandaged his wounds, pouring on olive oil and wine. Then he put him on his own animal, brought him to an inn, and took care of him.

- The oil of joy - the Holy Spirit. Isaiah 61:3 to provide for those who mourn in Zion; to give them a crown of beauty instead of ashes, festive oil instead of mourning, and splendid clothes instead of despair. And they will be called righteous trees, planted by the LORD to glorify Him.

- The illuminating lamp of the Holy Spirit. Matthew 25:3 When the foolish took their lamps, they didn't take olive oil with them.

- The consecrating oil - the Holy Spirit. Exodus 29:7 Take the anointing oil, pour it on his head, and anoint him.

5. The Holy Spirit is like rain and dew. Psalms 72:6 May He be like rain that falls on the cut grass, like spring showers that water the earth.

    - The fertilization of the Holy Spirit. Ezek. 34:26 I will make them and the area around My hill a blessing: I will send down showers in their season — showers of blessing.

    - The refreshing of the Holy Spirit. Psalms 68:9 You, God, showered abundant rain; You revived Your inheritance when it languished.

    - The abundance of the Holy Spirit. Psalms 133:3 It is like the dew of Hermon falling on the mountains of Zion. For there the LORD has appointed the blessing — life forevermore.

    - The imperceptibility of the Holy Spirit. 2 Samuel 17:12 Then we will attack David wherever we find him, and we will descend on him like dew on the ground. Not even one will be left of all the men with him

6. The Holy Spirit like a dove. Matthew 3:16 After Jesus was baptized, He went up immediately from the water. The heavens suddenly opened for Him, and He saw the Spirit of God descending like a dove and coming down on Him.

    - The gentleness of the Holy Spirit. Matthew 10:16 Look, I'm sending you out like sheep among wolves. Therefore be as shrewd as serpents and as harmless as doves.

BIBLE DOCTRINE

7. The Holy Spirit like a voice. Isaiah 6:8 Then I heard the voice of the Lord saying: Who should I send? Who will go for Us? I said: Here I am. Send me.

    - The speaking of the Holy Spirit. Matthew 10:20 because you are not speaking, but the Spirit of your Father is speaking through you.

    - The guidance of the Holy Spirit. Isaiah 30:21 and whenever you turn to the right or to the left, your ears will hear this command behind you: "This is the way. Walk in it.

    - The warnings of the Holy Spirit. Hebrews 3:7-11 Therefore, as the Holy Spirit says: Today, if you hear His voice, do not harden your hearts as in the rebellion,...

8. The Holy Spirit like a seal. Revelation 7:2 Then I saw another angel, who had the seal of the living God rise up from the east. He cried out in a loud voice to the four angels who were empowered to harm the earth and the sea:

    - The securing presence of the Holy Spirit. Ephesians 1:13 When you heard the message of truth, the gospel of your salvation, and when you believed in Him, you were also sealed with the promised Holy Spirit.

    - The authenticating of the Holy Spirit. John 6:27 Don't work for the food that perishes but for the food that lasts for eternal life, which the Son of Man will give you, because God the Father has set His seal of approval on Him.

9. The Holy Spirit like cloven tongues. Acts 2:3 And tongues, like flames of fire that were divided, appeared to them and rested on each one of them.

BIBLE DOCTRINE

The Ministries Of The Holy Spirit.

The Holy Spirit's ministries will forever exalt Jesus, convicting, regenerating, and dwelling within believers, sealing them for eternity. Guiding, prompting worship, empowering witness, enabling understanding of God's Word, and promising bodily resurrection. The Holy Spirit is an ever-present helper in our lives and is our best friend and His work in our life is unlimited, with a primary focus to transform us daily into His Image and likeness.

The Holy Spirit exalts Jesus. John 16:14 He will glorify Me, because He will take from what is Mine and declare it to you.

The Holy Spirit convicts us. John 16:8 When He comes, He will convict the world about sin, righteousness, and judgment:

The Holy Spirit regenerates us. John 3:5 Jesus answered, "I assure you: Unless someone is born of water and the Spirit, he cannot enter the kingdom of God.

The Holy Spirit lives in us. 1 Corinthians 6:19 Don't you know that your body is a sanctuary of the Holy Spirit who is in you, whom you have from God? You are not your own,

The Holy Spirit seals believers. Ephesians 1:13 When you heard the message of truth, the gospel of your salvation, and when you believed in Him, you were also sealed with the promised Holy Spirit.

The Holy Spirit teaches and guides us. John 14:26 But the Counselor, the Holy Spirit — the Father will send Him in My name — will teach you all things and remind you of everything I have told you.

The Holy Spirit is the Messenger of God. Isaiah 63:9 In all their suffering, He suffered, and the Angel of His Presence saved them. He redeemed them because of His love and compassion; He lifted them up and carried them all the days of the past.

The Holy Spirit is your helper. John 14:26 But the Counselor, the Holy Spirit — the Father will send Him in My name — will teach you all things and remind you of everything I have told you.

The Holy Spirit guides us to use our spiritual gift. 1 Corinthians 12:7 A demonstration of the Spirit is given to each person to produce what is beneficial:

The Spirit guides us into all truth. John 16:13 When the Spirit of truth comes, He will guide you into all the truth. For He will not speak on His own, but He will speak whatever He hears. He will also declare to you what is to come.

The Spirit reveals Christ to us and in us. John 16:14,15 He will glorify Me, because He will take from what is Mine and declare it to you. Everything the Father has is Mine. This is why I told you that He takes from what is Mine and will declare it to you.

The Spirit leads us. Matthew. 4:1 Then Jesus was led up by the Spirit into the wilderness to be tempted by the Devil.

The Holy Spirit leads us to be godly. Galatians 5:18 But if you are led by the Spirit, you are not under the law.

The Holy Spirit convicts people to change. John 16:8 When He comes, He will convict the world about sin, righteousness, and judgment:

The Holy Spirit compels us to worship. Ephesians 5:18 And don't get drunk with wine, which leads to reckless actions, but be filled by the Spirit:

The Holy Spirit prompts us to change our behavior Ephesians 4:30 And don't grieve God's Holy Spirit. You were sealed by Him for the day of redemption.

The Holy Spirit sanctifies us. Romans 15:16 to be a minister of Christ Jesus to the Gentiles, serving as a priest of God's good news. My purpose is that the offering of the Gentiles may be acceptable, sanctified by the Holy Spirit.

The Holy Spirit empowers us. Luke 4:14 Then Jesus returned to Galilee in the power of the Spirit, and news about Him spread throughout the entire vicinity.

The Holy Spirit fills us. Acts 2:4 Then they were all filled with the Holy Spirit and began to speak in different languages, as the Spirit gave them ability for speech.

The Holy Spirit teaches us to pray. Romans 8:26 In the same way the Spirit also joins to help in our weakness, because we do not know what to pray for as we should, but the Spirit Himself intercedes for us with unspoken groanings.

The Holy Spirit bears witness in us that we are children of God. Romans 8:16 The Spirit Himself testifies together with our spirit that we are God's children,

The Holy Spirit produces in us the fruit or evidence of His work and presence. Galatians 5:22,23 But the fruit of the Spirit is love, joy, peace, patience, kindness, goodness, faith, gentleness, self-control. Against such things there is no law.

The Holy Spirit distributes spiritual gifts and manifestations of His presence to and through the body. 1 Corinthians 12:4 Now there are different gifts, but the same Spirit.

The Holy Spirit anoints us for ministry. Luke 4:18 The Spirit of the Lord is on Me, because He has anointed Me to preach good news to the poor. He has sent Me to proclaim freedom to the captives and recovery of sight to the blind, to set free the oppressed,

The. Holy Spirit washes and renews us. Titus 3:5 He saved us — not by works of righteousness that we had done, but according to His mercy, through the washing of regeneration and renewal by the Holy Spirit.

The Holy Spirit brings unity to the body. Ephesians 4:3 diligently keeping the unity of the Spirit with the peace that binds us.

The Holy Spirit is our guarantee and deposit of the future resurrection. 2 Corinthians 1:22 He has also sealed us and given us the Spirit as a down payment in our hearts.

The Holy Spirit seals us for the day of redemption. Ephesians 1:13 When you heard the message of truth, the gospel of your salvation, and when you believed in Him, you were also sealed with the promised Holy Spirit.

The Holy Spirit sets us free from the law of sin and death. Romans 8:2 because the Spirit's law of life in Christ Jesus has set you free from the law of sin and of death.

The Holy Spirit quickens our mortal bodies. Romans 8:11 And if the Spirit of Him who raised Jesus from the dead lives in you, then He who raised Christ from the dead will also bring your mortal bodies to life through His Spirit who lives in you.

The Holy Spirit reveals the deep things of God to us. 1 Corinthians 2:10 Now God has revealed these things to us by the Spirit, for the Spirit searches everything, even the depths of God.

The Holy Spirit reveals what God has given us freely. 1 Corinthians 2:12 Now we have not received the spirit of the world, but the Spirit who comes from God, so that we may understand what has been freely given to us by God.

The Holy Spirit dwells in us. John 14:17 He is the Spirit of truth. The world is unable to receive Him because it doesn't see Him or know Him. But you do know Him, because He remains with you and will be in you.

The Holy Spirit speaks to, in, and through us. Acts 2:4 Then they were all filled with the Holy Spirit and began to speak in different languages, as the Spirit gave them the ability for speech.

The Holy Spirit is the agent by which we are baptized into the body of Christ. 1 Corinthians 12:13 For we were all baptized by one Spirit into one body — whether Jews or Greeks, whether slaves or free — and we were all made to drink of one Spirit.

The Holy Spirit brings liberty. 2 Corinthians 3:17 Now the Lord is the Spirit, and where the Spirit of the Lord is, there is freedom.

The Holy Spirit transforms us into the image of Christ. 2 Corinthians 3:18 We all, with unveiled faces, are looking as in a mirror at the glory of the Lord and are being transformed into the same image from glory to glory; this is from the Lord who is the Spirit.

The Holy Spirit cries in our hearts, "Abba! Father. Galatians 4:6 And because you are sons, God has sent the Spirit of His Son into our hearts, crying, "Abba, Father!"

The Holy Spirit enables us to wait. Galatians 5:5 For through the Spirit, by faith, we eagerly wait for the hope of righteousness.

The Holy Spirit supplies us with Christ. Philippians 1:19

The Holy Spirit grants everlasting life. Galatians 6:8 because the one who sows to his flesh will reap corruption from the flesh, but the one who sows to the Spirit will reap eternal life from the Spirit.

The Holy Spirit gives us access to God the Father. Ephesians 2:18 For through Him we both have access by one Spirit to the Father.

The Holy Spirit makes us God's habitation. Ephesians 2:22 You also are being built together for God's dwelling in the Spirit.

The Holy Spirit reveals the mystery of God to us. Ephesians 3:4,5 y reading this you are able to understand my insight about the mystery of the Messiah. This was not made known to people in other generations as it is now revealed to His holy apostles and prophets by the Spirit:

The Holy Spirit strengthens our spirits. Ephesians 3:16 I pray that He may grant you, according to the riches of His glory, to be strengthened with power in the inner man through His Spirit,

The Holy Spirit enables us to obey the truth. 1 Peter 1:22 By obedience to the truth, having purified yourselves for sincere love of the brothers, love one another earnestly from a pure heart,

The Holy Spirit enables us to know that Jesus abides in us. 1 John 3:24 The one who keeps His commands remains in Him, and He in him. And the way we know that He remains in us is from the Spirit He has given us.

The Holy Spirit confesses that Jesus came in the flesh. 1 John 4:2 This is how you know the Spirit of God: Every spirit who confesses that Jesus Christ has come in the flesh is from God.

The Spirit says, "Come, Lord Jesus," along with the bride. Revelations 22:17 Both the Spirit and the bride say, "Come!" Anyone who hears should say, "Come!" And the one who is thirsty should come. Whoever desires should take the living water as a gift.

The Holy Spirit pours out God's love into our hearts. Romans 5:5 This hope will not disappoint us, because God's love has been poured out in our hearts through the Holy Spirit who was given to us.

The Spirit bears witness to the truth in our conscience. Romans 9:1 I speak the truth in Christ — I am not lying; my conscience is testifying to me with the Holy Spirit

The Holy Spirit teaches us. John 14:26 But the Counselor, the Holy Spirit — the Father will send Him in My name — will teach you all things and remind you of everything I have told you.

The Holy Spirit gives us joy. 1 Thessalonians 1:6 and you became imitators of us and of the Lord when, in spite of severe persecution, you welcomed the message with joy from the Holy Spirit.

The Holy Spirit enables some to preach the gospel. 1 Peter 1:12 It was revealed to them that they were not serving themselves but you. These things have now been announced to you through those who preached the gospel to you by the Holy Spirit sent from heaven. Angels desire to look into these things.

The Holy Spirit moves us. 2 Peter 1:21 because no prophecy ever came by the will of man; instead, men spoke from God as they were moved by the Holy Spirit.

The Holy Spirit knows the thoughts of God. 1 Corinthians 2:11 For who among men knows the thoughts of a man except the spirit of the man that is in him? In the same way, no one knows the thoughts of God except the Spirit of God.

The Holy Spirit casts out demons. Matthew 12:28 If I drive out demons by the Spirit of God, then the kingdom of God has come to you.

The Holy Spirit brings things to our remembrance. John 14:26 But the Counselor, the Holy Spirit — the Father will send Him in My name — will teach you all things and remind you of everything I have told you.

The Holy Spirit comforts us. Acts 9:31 So the church throughout all Judea, Galilee, and Samaria had peace, being built up and walking in the fear of the Lord and in the encouragement of the Holy Spirit, and it increased in numbers.

The Gifts And Fruit Of The Holy Spirit

Holy Spirit has two manifestations of His Glory and they are, Gifts and Fruit.

The Gifts of Holy Spirit are given by The Holy Spirit to show the Glory of God, for the edification of others, and for the believer who carries the gift.

Fruit of Holy Spirit is developed in a believer when the believer is abiding in Christ.

Fruit of The Holy Spirit can diminish in a believer when the believer is not abiding in Christ.

A non-believer does not and cannot have and fruit of Holy Spirit. Though a person who was in Christ and filled with the Holy Spirt, then falls away from Christ, will still retain their gift of the Holy Spirit as the gifts of the Holy Spirit are without repentance and are never taken away.
No two gifts and no two fruits of the Holy Spirit are the same, and generally, no twobelievers have exactly the same gifts and fruit in their lives.
The gifts of Holy Spirit can never be taken away, though the fruit of Holy Spirit can be lost, removed and taken away.

Fruit of Holy Spirit	Gifts of Holy Spirit
1. Love	1. Words of wisdom
2. Joy	2. Word of knowledge
3. Peace	3. Prophecy

BIBLE DOCTRINE

4.	Patience	4.	Faith
5.	Kindness	5.	Healing
6.	Goodness	6.	Miracle
7.	Faithfulness	7.	Discerning of spirits
8.	Gentleness	8.	Different kinds of tongues
9.	Self-control	9.	Interpretation of tongues

Romans 11:29 "The gifts and calling of God are without repentance."

"Without repentance" means that God won't change His mind about what He has called you to do even if you turn away from God.

If God has called you, that calling is still there, whether or not you obey God. Gifts and calling were first given long before the creation of the earth, and long before man was even created.

The 1st gifts and calling given, were given to the Archangels, Michael, Gabriel andLucifer.

1. Michael the Archangel was given the calling of commander of God's army and gifted with power and authority, who protects the people of God.

BIBLE DOCTRINE

2. Gabriel the Archangel was given the calling of being the official messenger of God and gifted with standing in the presence of God.

3. Lucifer the Archangel was given beauty, wisdom, wealth and responsibility of the worship of Heaven. Ezekiel 28. Though Lucifer still has all these gifts he is rotten to the core. When Lucifer fell, God never took away these three gifts.

Romans 8:14 We are not called to follow or our gifting or our calling, we are called to follow Spirit of God.

Matthew 7:11 The Word of the Lord says our Father has given to us good gifts.

2 Timothy 1:6 Paul told Timothy to "stir up" the gift that was to him

Gifts Of Holy Spirit

The nine gifts of The Holy Spirit are divided into 3 categories:

1. Revelation gifts are gifts that knows the unknown.
    a. Word of wisdom is information of the past.
    b. Word of knowledge is information of the present.
    c. Discerning of spirits is spiritual discerning, that is a gift of The Holy Spirit, while natural discerning is taught and inherited.

2. Power gifts are gifts that do things and performs actions.
    a. Gift of faith is faith above normal faith.
    b. Gift of healing have no variables or limitations, they are for body, soul, or spirit.
    c. Miracles are the authority of the elements and situations in life.

3. Utterance gifts are gift that make declarations.
    a. Prophecy is information of the future.
    b. Speaking in tongues is declaring in your Heavenly language.
    c. Interpretation of tongues is the Spirit language that can only be interpreted.

BIBLE DOCTRINE

The nine gifts of The Holy Spirit are:

1. Words of wisdom is information that comes from The Holy Spirit and relates to past-tense circumstances in life.

2. Words of knowledge is present-tense information that comes from The Holy Spirit.

3. The gift of faith is extra-ordinary confidence in God's promises.
It is the gift that exudes confidence in all situations.
It is the gift of optimism beyond the natural.
It is a gift and not a virtue that can be worked up by human effort.
It is a gift that involves belief but it goes beyond human believing because it involves the personal revelation and in working of God.
It is the gift that is always God's work.

4. The gift of healing is the manifestation of the power of God in the area of disease or dis-ease.
Sometimes the Holy Spirit will not give healing to some people who seem to need healing.
There are several reasons for this;
   - Unbelief. Mark 9:24 Immediately the father of the boy cried out, "I do believe! Help my unbelief."

- Failure to relate properly to the body. 1 Corinthians 11:29 For whoever eats and drinks without recognizing the body, eats and drinks judgment on himself.

- Special reasons. 2 Corinthians 12:7 especially because of the extraordinary revelations. Therefore, so that I would not exalt myself, a thorn in the flesh was given to me, a messenger of Satan to torment me so I would not exalt myself.

5. The gift of miracles is the explosive supernatural power to do things that are otherwise impossible that alters, suspends or in some other way controls the laws of nature.

6. The gift of prophecy is the gift to foretell, forthtell, predict, correct encourage, exhort and edify.

   The gift of prophecy is a gift of the Holy Spirit, and is not to be confused with the office of a prophet, or simply being prophetic.

   The gift of prophecy is not the office of the prophet. 1 Corinthians 12:10 to another, the performing of miracles, to another, prophecy, to another, distinguishing between spirits, to another, different kinds of languages, to another, interpretation of languages.

   The gift of prophecy should be the most desired gift. 1 Corinthians 14:1 Pursue love and desire spiritual gifts, and above all that you may prophesy.

The gift of prophecy should be the most edifying gift. 1 Corinthians 14:3 But the person who prophesies speaks to people for edification, encouragement, and consolation.

The gift of prophecy cannot be earned. 1 Corinthians 4:7 Even inanimate things that produce sounds — whether flute or harp — if they don't make a distinction in the notes, how will what is played on the flute or harp be recognized?

7. The gift of discernment is looking beyond the outward to the inward, seeing right through.

   The gift of discernment is to know the motivations and intentions before actions have been applied.

   The discerning of spirits, is to look beyond the natural and into the spiritual.

8. Speaking in tongues bypasses all-natural reasoning and connects you to the Spirit of God.

   When you speak in tongues you speak the mysteries of God.

   When you speak in tongues you don't know about things that the Holy Spirit knows about and the Holy Spirit desires to bring revelation to you on these issues concerning you and concerning things that He has for your future.

   The use of the gift of interpretation and interpret speaking in tongues is to bring revelation to your soul.

There are 4 reasons you speak in tongues:

   1) Sign to the unbeliever.

   2) Heavenly communication.

   3) Worship and warfare (Personal)

   4) Self-encouragement. (Personal)

9. The gift of interpretation of tongues is to give the meaning of what The Holy Spirit has spoken.

    The purpose for the gift of interpretation is to build up the Body of Christ by giving the meaning of what was being spoken.

    The edification comes through the revelation of the interpretation.

Fruit Of Holy Spirit:

1 Corinthians 12:8-11 to one is given a message of wisdom through the Spirit, to another, a message of knowledge by the same Spirit, to another, faith by the same Spirit, to another, gifts of healing by the one Spirit, to another, the performing of miracles, to another, prophecy, to another, distinguishing between spirits, to another, different kinds of languages, to another, interpretation of languages.

Galatians 5:22-23 But the fruit of the Spirit is love, joy, peace, longsuffering, gentleness, goodness, faith, meekness, temperance: against such there is no law.

The desire of God for your life is for you to bear spiritual fruit through your relationship to Jesus Christ.

The fruit of the Holy Spirit comes to us as a small seed which must be nurtured and developed in your life through prayer, reading the Word and by putting your faith into action.

The Bible begins and ends with talking about fruit.
Genesis 2:15-16 Of every tree of the garden you may freely eat: except from the tree of the knowledge of good and evil.

Revelation 22:1-2 And on this side of the river and on that was the tree of life, bearing twelve manner of fruits, yielding its fruit every month: and the leaves of the tree were for the healing of the nations.

God is the divine gardener and bearing fruit is a supernatural process that must take place in your life.

You must bear fruit or your branches will be cut and destroyed by fire.
John 15:1-2 I am the true vine, and my Father is the husbandman. Every branch in me that does not bear fruit will be taken away: and every branch that bears fruit will be pruned so that it may bring forth more fruit.

The nine fruit of Holy Spirit are divided into 3 categories:

1. Fruit that focuses on your relationship with God.
   Love – Joy - Peace
2. Fruit that focuses on your relationship with others.
   Longsuffering - Gentleness - Goodness
3. Fruit that is self-focused.
   Faith - Meekness - Temperance

The nine fruit of the holy spirit:

1. Fruit of Love. The fruit of Love is possibly the most misused and misunderstood word in all cultures.

    Love is the greatest of fruit and should be desired.

    1 Corinthians 13;4-7 Love is patient, love is kind. Love does not envy, is not boastful, is not conceited, does not act improperly, is not selfish, is not provoked, and does not keep a record of wrongs. Love finds no joy in unrighteousness but rejoices in the truth. It bears all things, believes all things, hopes all things, endures all things.

    There are 3 common Greek words used for love.

    a. Eros love; Sensual sexual attraction and desire. Eros is not found in the N.T.

    b. Philia love is the Brother / Sister love.

    c. Agape God's love.

2. Fruit of Joy. The fruit of Joy is not an emotion, it is a fruit of the Holy Spirit.

    Happiness is an emotion and dependent on circumstances.

    Joy is independent of circumstances.

    Joy is expressed in 3 ways:

    1. Singing joyfully
    2. Shouting with the voice of triumph
    3. Dancing in victory

    Joy is an expression of the Holy Spirit in your life.

    Laughter in the Holy Spirit is the Joy of The Lord.

There 4 words to define Joy in Aramaic

1. Gil – Joy at God's works.
2. Ranan – Shouts of joy over God's saving works.
3. Sus – Enthusiasm in God and His Word.
4. Samah – Joyfull disposition.

There are 3 words to define Joy in Greek

1. Agalliao: Loud, public expression of joy in worship
2. Euphraino: Community joy.
3. Chairo: To rejoice exceedingly

3. Fruit of Peace. The fruit of Peace is righteousness, peace and joy in your life.

    Battles are won through the fruit of peace. - God of Peace will crush satan under your feet. Romans 16:20

    Jesus said 'My peace I give to you'. John 14:27 & Eph 2:14

    Peace must be your plumb-line Colossians 3:15

    The fruit of peace is all about your plumbline.

    Peace must rule in your storm.

4. Fruit of Patience. The fruit of patience longsuffering and steadfastness in obedience to God, despite pressure to deny Him.

    Patience is the ability to withhold what you want, not just among other people, but yourself.

    Devil does not want you to have patience.

    The test of patience comes when your rights are violated.

    When everything is going your way, patience is easy to demonstrate.

5. 5 and 6 Fruit of goodness and fruit of kindness are sometimes used interchangeably.

6. Fruit of goodness and kindness is beautiful, attractive, useful, profitable, desirable and morally right

7. Fruit of self-control is the fruit that will enable you to master your desires and passions, especially your sensual appetites.

Self-control is enkrateaia and this is to have power.

No self-control is akrasia and no self-control renders one to be powerless and overwhelmed by passions.

Self-control brings honor to yourself and Glory to God.

8. 8 and 9 Fruit of meekness and gentleness are sometimes interchangeable. Both fruit of meekness and gentleness are power under control.

Meekness is a submitted attitude of gratitude.

9. Self-centeredness produces anger and violence. Meekness produces gentleness.

The Holy Spirit Your Helper

THE HOLY SPIRIT is your Ezer kenegdo

THE HOLY SPIRIT is your Eli-Ezer

- Eli means my God.
- Ezer means my helper.
- Ezer is qualified by the word Kenegdo in Genesis 2:18, 20.
- Kenegdo is translated as suitable for him.

John 14:26 'But the Helper (Ezer), the Holy Spirit, whom the Father will send in my name, he will teach you all things and bring to your remembrance all that I have said to you.'

The first time the title Ezer was used was in Genesis 2;18 'Then the Lord God said, "It is not good for the man to be alone. I will make a helper (Ezer / Kenegdo) as his complement.'

Ezer is used 21 times in the Old Testament.

    2 x for woman as a helper

    16 x for God being your helper

    3 x for a negative context

Ezer was the word to describe the first woman.

Eve was Adams helper / Ezer / Kenegdo.

The Word Ezer / Kenegdo that was used for Eve is the same word as Ezer that's used for the Holy Spirit.

Ezer describes aspects of personality of the Holy Spirit:

The Holy Spirit is our strength.

The Holy Spirit is our rescuer.

The Holy Spirit is our protector.

The Holy Spirit is our helper.

Exodus 18:3-4 Moses was prophetic in naming his children Eli-ezer and Gershom.

- Eli-Ezer means God is my helper
- Gershom means sojourner and a pilgrim.

Fellowship, Friendship, And Benefits With The Holy Spirit

Philippians 2:1 If then there is any encouragement in Christ, if any consolation of love, if any fellowship with the Spirit, if any affection and mercy,

The definition for fellowship of the Holy Spirit is:

- Intimate friendship.
- Community.

- Experiencing a deepening relationship.
- Extreme level of closeness, intimacy and communication.

Fellowship in Greek is Koinonia (koihn-ee'-ah) and it means partnership, communication, communion and intimate fellowship.

Without the Holy Spirit, we have;
1. No victory over sin.
2. No intimacy and revelation with God.
3. No spiritual discernment or wisdom.
4. No spiritual gifts or fruit.
5. No resurrection from the dead and eternal life.

Eight steps to deepen your relationship with the Holy Spirit
1. Seek His Presence.
2. Desire His anointing. John 7:37-39
3. Find the resting place of God.
4. Build an altar through prayer and Study His Word.   John 6:63
5. Ask The Holy Spirit to remove all hinderances in your life that stop you from seeking Him and experiencing His anointing.

BIBLE DOCTRINE

Five benefits of Fellowship of the Holy Spirit

1. True worship reveals true worshipers.
2. Revelation flows from intimacy.
3. Restoration and renewal.
4. Empowered and enabled.
5. Carry the Anointing and Glory of God.

BIBLE DOCTRINE

DOCTRINE OF THE BIBLE

Hebrews 4:12 For the word of God (Jesus) is alive and active. Sharper than any double-edged sword, it penetrates even to dividing soul and spirit, joints and marrow; it judges the thoughts and attitudes of the heart.

2 Timothy 3:16,17 All Scripture is God-breathed and is useful for teaching, rebuking, correcting and training in righteousness, so that the servant of God may be thoroughly equipped for every good work.

The Bible is the Word of God through revelation.
The Bible is the Word of God through inspiration.
The Bible is the Word of God through illumination.

The Bible is the world's best-selling book of all times every year.
The Bible has sold over fifty million copies and has sales over 50 Bibles that are sold every minute of the day, every year, year after year.

The Bible in Greek is Biblion means book or scroll, and is also known as Hagio the Holy Books. The root word biblion is byblos, the papyrus plant, from which early scrolls were made.

The Holy Bible in Anglo-Latin is Biblia Sacra and means Holy Books.

BIBLE DOCTRINE

The Bible was given through revelation from God to man.

The Bible was brought together in three ways:

1. Revelation. From God to man. Revelation 1:1 The revelation of Jesus Christ that God gave Him to show His slaves what must quickly take place. He sent it and signified it through His angel to His slave John,
2. Inspiration. From God through man into written form. Matthew 4:4 But He answered, "It is written: Man must not live on bread alone but on every word that comes from the mouth of God."
3. Illumination. From God through the Bible to man. Psalms 119:105 Your word is a lamp for my feet and a light on my path.

There Are Eight Ways God Reveals His Word:

1. God reveals His Word through His audible voice. Genesis 3:9 So the LORD God called out to the man and said to him, "Where are you?"
2. God reveals His Word through His gentle soft voice. 1 Kings 19:12 After the earthquake there was a fire, but the LORD was not in the fire. And after the fire there was a voice, a soft whisper.
3. God reveals His Word through Christophanies also known as Theophanie. Genesis 16:7 The Angel of the LORD found her by a spring of water in the wilderness, the spring on the way to Shur.

4. God reveals His Word through Angels. Acts 8:26 n angel of the Lord spoke to Philip: "Get up and go south to the road that goes down from Jerusalem to Gaza." (This is the desert road.)

5. God reveals His Word through nature. Psalms 19:2 Day after day they pour out speech; night after night they communicate knowledge.

6. God reveals His Word through an animal. Numbers 22:28 Then the LORD opened the donkey's mouth, and she asked Balaam, "What have I done to you that you have beaten me these three times?"

7. God reveals His Word through dreams. Genesis 28:13 Yahweh was standing there beside him, saying, "I am Yahweh, the God of your father Abraham and the God of Isaac. I will give you and your offspring the land that you are now sleeping on.

8. God reveals His Word through visions. Acts 10:3-6 When the angel who spoke to him had gone, he called two of his household slaves and a devout soldier, who was one of those who attended him.

The Supreme Authority Of The Bible:

2 Timothy 3:16 All Scripture is given by inspiration of God, and is profitable for doctrine, for reproof, for correction, for instruction in righteousness.

The Bible is the supreme authority of The Word of God, revealing its infallibility and cannot fail to communicate the Truth of all that God wants to reveal. The inerrancy of The Word God reveals to us that the Bible cannot in any way contradict itself in written form through the inspired Words of God and focuses on the specific details in both thoughts and concepts. The Word of God in its infallibility cannot be wrong and The Word of God in its inerrancy cannot make a mistake.

Quote by Charles H. Spurgeon. If I did not believe in the infallibility of this book I would rather be without it. If I am to judge the book it is no judge of me. If I am to sift it and lay this aside and only accept that according to my own judgment, then I have no guidance whatever unless I have conceit enough to trust my own heart. The new theory denies the infallibility of the words of God but is practically imputed to the judgments of men. At least this is all the infallibility that they can get at. I protest that I would rather risk my soul with a God-inspired Word from heaven than with differing leaders who arise from the earth at the core of modern thoughts.

Writings That Were Not Included In The Bible.

The Bible declares that all scripture is God-breathed, and we see that those who received the inspiration to record the Word of The Lord did so under Divine inspiration.

2 Timothy 3:16 All Scripture is inspired by God...

2 Peter 1:20,21 No prophecy of Scripture comes from one's own interpretation, because no prophecy ever came by the will of man; instead, men spoke from God as they were moved by the Holy Spirit.

Luke 1:70 Just as He spoke by the mouth of His holy prophets in ancient times;

During the Old Testament period, a number of books were composed, that were not Divinely inspired, and for that reason they were not included into the Bible. The writer of the Book of Ecclesiastes made the following admission about the making of books:

Ecclesiastes 12:12 "Of anything beyond these, my child, beware. Of making many books there is no end, and much study is a weariness of the flesh.

Some of the books not in Scripture are
1. The Book of the Wars of the Lord. Numbers 21:14 Book of the Wars of the Lord.
2. The Book of Jasher. (the scroll of the upright One) Joshua 10:13 And the sun stood still and the moon stopped until the nation took vengeance on its enemies. Isn't this written in the Book of Jashar?
3. Solomon's Proverbs and Songs. 1 Kings 4:32,33 He spoke three thousand proverbs and his songs numbered a thousand and five. He described plant life, from the cedar of Lebanon to the hyssop that

grows out of walls. He also taught about animals and birds, reptiles and fish. (The Book of Proverbs does not contain three thousand proverbs. The Song of Solomon is the only part of Scripture that contains a song from Solomon. For some reason, many of the proverbs and the songs of Solomon were not placed in Holy Scripture.)

4. The Acts of Solomon (The Annals of Solomon.) 1 Kings 11:41 As for the other events of Solomon's reign - all he did and the wisdom he displayed - are they not written in the book of the annals of Solomon?

5. The Annals of the Kings of Israel. 1 Kings 14:19 The other events of Jeroboam's reign, his wars and how he ruled, are written in the book of the annals of the kings of Israel.

6. The Annals of the Kings of Judah. 1 Kings 15:7 As for the other events of Abijah's reign, and all he did, are they not written in the book of the annals of the kings of Judah? There was war between Abijah and Jeroboam.

7. The writings of Nathan and Gad. 1 Chronicles 29:29 As for the events of King David's reign, from beginning to end, they are written in the records of Samuel the seer, the records of Nathan the prophet and the records of Gad the seer.

8. And again about Nathan the prophet. 2 Chronicles 9:29 As for the other events of Solomon's reign, from beginning to end, are they not written in the records of Nathan the prophet, in the prophecy

of Ahijah the Shilonite and in the visions of Iddo the seer concerning Jeroboam son of Nebat?

9. Along with Nathan, there is mention of other writings: the prophecy of Ahijah, and the vision of Iddo the seer. Again, we know nothing else of these writings.

9. The Records of Shemaiah the Prophet and Iddo the Seer

10. A prophet named Shemaiah, and a seer named Iddo. 2 Chronicles 12:15 The events of Rehoboam's reign, from beginning to end, are written in the Events of Shemaiah the Prophet and of Iddo the Seer concerning genealogies. There was war between Rehoboam and Jeroboam throughout their reigns.

11. The Acts of Uzziah, written by Amoz, the son Isaiah. 2 Chronicles 26:22 Now the prophet Isaiah son of Amoz wrote about the rest of the events of Uzziah's reign, from beginning to end.

12. The Laments of the Dirges. 2 Chronicles 35:25 Jeremiah chanted a dirge over Josiah, and all the singing men and singing women still speak of Josiah in their dirges to this very day. They established them as a statute for Israel, and indeed they are written in the Dirges.

13. Samuel wrote the rights and duties of kingship. 1 Samuel 10:25

In the New Testament period, several books were composed, that were not included and were not the express word of God, and most times were added on through the papal era. These books have come to light and are called 'lost books'. The early Church fathers heavily influenced what would be considered Scripture and what would be rejected, as they were trusted men of God like Polycarp, Justin Martyr, Tertullian, Origen, Eusebius, Athanasius, Jerome, and Augustine who led the slow, careful acceptance of the books of the New Testament.

The so-called "lost books" of the Bible are forgeries and figments of the author's imagination and were never accepted as canonical or scriptural. They are recent in origin and cannot be traced back to the 1st-century church.

The so-called lost books were introduced into society many years after the New Testament Books were established to be The Word of God. They were the writings of scholars and heretics who read the Secrets of Enoch, the Conflict of Adam and Eve with Satan, The Psalms of Solomon 4, and alleged gospels by Philip, the Apocalypse of Peter, and the Gospel of Mary. These scholars and heretics could easily have discerned that the so-called lost books were not consistent with the 66 books of the Bible, and were not the inspired Word of God.

These books would not and could fit in contextually or doctrinally into the Bible.

Many other books such as 1 Maccabees, the Wisdom of Solomon, and other such books are what we call the Apocrypha and were never placed into the Bible as we know it today, as they were rejected by the Jews. Although these extra-biblical books may have some accurate historical accounts, God, in His sovereignty, did not cause them to be accepted as His inspired Words and so they too were not included in the Bible.

The Apostle Paul warned us in Galatians 1:8 'But even if we or an angel from heaven should preach to you a gospel other than what we have preached to you, a curse be on him!'. And in Romans 16:17,18 Now I urge you, brothers, to watch out for those who cause dissensions and obstacles contrary to the doctrine you have learned. Avoid them, for such people do not serve our Lord Christ but their own appetites. They deceive the hearts of the unsuspecting with smooth talk and flattering words.

Deception is subtle and slowly changes the truth to a lie.

In 2 Corinthians 11:4 Paul writes, 'For if a person comes and preaches another Jesus, whom we did not preach, or you receive a different spirit, which you had not received, or a different gospel, which you had not accepted, you put up with it splendidly!'

The Apostle John tells us that not every spirit is from God in 1 John 4:1, "Beloved, do not believe every spirit, but test the spirits to see whether they are from God because many false prophets have gone out into the world." And then he goes on to say in verse 6, "We are from God; he who knows God listens to us; he who is not from God does not listen to us. By this, we know the spirit of truth and the spirit of error."

In the Sermon on the Mount, Jesus warns about false prophets who sow seeds of deception. They are genuinely deceptive and highly dangerous. Jesus says they come in sheep's clothing, but inwardly they're ferocious wolves. They come to twist the Truth and like Lucifer coming to Eve and saying, 'Did God really say ...'

It is most important to hold onto the Truth. 1 John 2:24 What you have heard from the beginning must remain in you. If what you have heard from the beginning remains in you, then you will remain in the Son and in the Father.

Over-View The 66 Books Of The Bible

The Old Testament was written in Aramaic on five different elements:

1. Clay; Jeremiah 17:13 LORD, the hope of Israel, all who abandon You will be put to shame All who turn away from Me will be written in the dirt, for they have abandoned the LORD, the fountain of living water.
2. Stone; Exodus 24:12 The LORD said to Moses, "Come up to Me on the mountain and stay there so that I may give you the stone tablets with the law and commandments I have written for their instruction."
3. Papyrus; 2 John 12 Though I have many things to write to you, I don't want to do so with paper and ink. Instead, I hope to be with you and talk face to face so that our joy may be complete.
4. Vellum (calf skin) and parchment (lamb skin); 2 Timothy 4:13 When you come, bring the cloak I left in Troas with Carpus, as well as the scrolls, especially the parchments.

5. Metal; Exodus 28:36 "You are to make a pure gold medallion and engrave it, like the engraving of a seal:

The Old Testament has thirty-nine book, divided into four categories:

Five Books of the Law known as the Pentateuch or Torah.

1. Genesis: Explains creation, Fall of man, Flood, Tower of Babe, and the call of Abraham.
2. Exodus: The call of Moses, the Passover, the Red Sea Crossing, the giving of the Sabbath, the giving of the law, and at the completion of the Tabernacle.
3. Leviticus: The anointing of Aaron as Israel's first high priest, the feasts of Israel and the ceremonial law.
4. Numbers: The rebellion at Kaddish Barnea, the serpent of Brass the census of the people and wanderings in the wilderness.
5. Deuteronomy: Israel is future predicted by Moses and his death.

The 12 Books of History.

6. Joshua: Israel enters the promised land and the partition of the land.
7. Judges; The rule of the judges and the history of the nation from Joshua to Samson.
8. Ruth: The marriage of Boaz and Ruth and the story of the royal family of Judah.

9. 1 Samuel: The anointing of Saul Israel's first king and the anointing of David to become future king during the judgeship of Samuel.
10. 2 Samuel: Jerusalem becomes the capital of Israel and the giving of the Davidic covenant under the reign of David.
11. 1 Kings: The dedication of the temple by Solomon and the divided kingdom of Israel.
12. 2 Kings: The capture of the northern kingdom by Assyria and the capture of the southern kingdom by Babylon.
13. 1 Chronicles: The official history of Judah and Israel.
14. 2 Chronicles: The official history of Judah and Israel.
15. Ezra: The decree of Cyrus and the return to Jerusalem and the temple.
16. Nehemiah: The rebuilding of the wall and the temple and the temple.
17. Esther: Is a prophetic type of the present day Church married to Christ.

Five Books of Wisdom which are poetry and praise.

18. Job deals with the meaning of life, the existence of evil and our relationship to God.
19. Psalms contain many sayings of practical wisdom to help live a happy, successful and holy life.
20. Proverbs contain many sayings of practical wisdom to help live a happy, successful and holy life.
21. Ecclesiastes deals with the meaning of life, the existence of evil, and our relationship to God.

22. Song of Songs is a love song between a man and woman interpreted as a story about the love of God for Israel and the Church.

The 5 Books of the Major Prophets (longer in message) and the 12 books of the Minor Prophets (shorter in message).

Major Prophets:

23. Isaiah: Each chapter covers all 66 books of the Bible in chronological order.
24. Jeremiah: Prophecies announcing the captivity of Judah, its sufferings, and the overthrow of their enemy.
25. Lamentations: The utterance of Jeremiah's sorrow upon the capture of Jerusalem and the destruction of the temple
26. Ezekiel: Messages of warning and comfort to the Jews in their captivity.
27. Daniel: The occurrences of the captivity, and a series of prophecies concerning Christ.

Minor Prophets

28. Hosea: Prophecies relating to Christ and the latter days
29. Joel: Prophecy of woes upon Judah, and of the favor with which God will receive the penitent people and most of all the outpouring of The Holy Spirit on all flesh.
30. Amos: Prophecy that Israel and other neighboring nations will be punished by conquerors from the north, and of the fulfillment of the Messiah's kingdom.

31. Obadiah: Prophecy of the desolation of Edom.

32. Jonah: His disobedience to God, the whale and salvation to Nineveh.

33. Micah: Prophecy relating to the invasions of Shalmaneser and Sennacherib, the Babylonish captivity, the establishment of a theocratic kingdom in Jerusalem, and the birth of the Messiah in Bethlehem.

34. Nahum: Prophecy of the downfall of Assyria.

35. Habakkuk: Prophecy of the doom of the Chaldeans.

36. Zephaniah: Prophecy of the overthrow of Judah for its idolatry and wickedness.

37. Haggai: Prophecies concerning the rebuilding of the temple.

38. Zechariah: Prophecies relating to the rebuilding of the temple and the Messiah.

39. Malachi: Prophecies relating to the calling of the Gentiles and the coming of Christ.

After 4 centuries of silence where the Bible does not record a prophetic Word from God, a new prophet, John the Baptist, arrived to prepare the way for the long-awaited Messiah, whom he identified as Jesus.

God provided the ultimate redemption plan for His people and all mankind by giving the gift of His Son, Jesus – who is both human and God, born of the virgin Mary.

On the revelation and understanding of Jesus Christ, who is The Rock on which the Church is built, the entire New Testament unfolds with twenty-seven Books that are divided into four categories written entirely in Greek, though parts of the messages of Jesus were spoken in Aramaic.

The New Testament was written on papyrus, pottery chards, stone, clay and wax tablets

Over-View Of The New Testament

The Gospels

40. Matthew: A brief history of the life of Christ.
41. Mark: A brief history of the life of Christ, supplying some incidents omitted by St. Matthew.
42. Luke: The history of the life of Christ, with special reference to his most important acts and discourses.
43. John: The life of Christ, giving important discourses not related by the other evangelists.

The Early Church History

44. Acts: The actions of the early church in the power of The Holy Spirit.

BIBLE DOCTRINE

The letters to the Early Church. As churches were established in different cities, Jesus' disciples wrote letters (today known as books of the New Testament), under the inspiration of The Holy Spirit to instruct those believers, and us, on how to live as a follower of Jesus.

45. Romans: A treatise by St. Paul on the doctrine of justification by Christ.
46. 1 Corinthians: A letter from St. Paul to the Corinthians, correcting errors into which they had fallen.
47. 2 Corinthians: St. Paul confirms his disciples in their faith, and vindicates his own character.
48. Galatians: St. Paul maintains that we are justified by faith, and not by rites.
49. Ephesians: A treatise by St. Paul on the power of divine grace.
50. Philippians: St. Paul sets forth the beauty of Christian kindness.
51. Colossians: St. Paul warns his disciples against errors, and exhorts to certain duties.
52. 1 Thessalonians: St. Paul exhorts his disciples to continue in the faith and in holy conversation.
53. 2 Thessalonians: St. Paul corrects an error concerning the speedy coming of Christ the second time.
54. 1 Timothy: St. Paul instructs Timothy in the duty of a pastor, and encourages him in the work of the ministry.
55. 2 Timothy: The message is a continuation from 1 Timothy
56. Titus: St. Paul encourages Titus in the performance of his ministerial duties.

57. Philemon: An appeal to a converted master to receive a converted escaped slave with kindness.
58. Hebrews: St. Paul maintains that Christ is the substance of the ceremonial law.
59. James: A treatise on the efficacy of faith united with good works.
60. 1 Peter: Exhortations to a Christian life, with various warnings and predictions.
61. 2 Peter: The message is a continuation from 1 Peter.
62. 1 John: Respecting the person of our Lord, and an exhortation to Christian love and conduct.
63. 2 John: St. John warns a converted lady against false teachers.
64. 3 John: A letter to Gaius, praising him for his hospitality.
65. Jude: Warnings against deceivers.

The Apocalyptic Prophecy

66. Revelation.

> Written by John on the Isle of Patmos, this is the last letter in the New Testament captures a vision, which explains Jesus' return and the end of the earth. It is in these last days, when Jesus returns, where our redemption will be completed and communion with God will be permanently restored for humankind.

BIBLE DOCTRINE

Bible Timeline

Old Testament Era - BC (Before Christ)

4000   The earliest recordings were orally handed down.

2000 - 1400   The Book of Job – possibly written by Moses.

1400   The 10 Commandments on stone tablets given to Moses at Mount Sinai, later stored in the Ark of the Covenant.

1402   Pentateuch

1350   Joshua before

1050   Judges and Ruth

965   Psalms

926   Proverbs, Ecclesiastes, son of Solomon

926   1 & 2 Samuel

848   1 & 2 Kings and 1 & 2 Chronicles

848   Obadiah

835   Joel

780   Jonah

765   Amos

755   Hosea

750   Isaiah

740   Micah

640   Jeremiah and Lamentations

630   Nahum

625   Habakkuk and Zephaniah

593	Ezekiel
539	1 & 2 Kings and 1 & 2 chronicles before
538	Daniel before
520	Haggai and Zachariah
476	Esther
558	Ezra
445	Nehemiah
432	Malachi
300	All of the original Old Testament Hebrew books have been written, collected, and recognized as official, canonical books.
250–200	The Septuagint, The Greek translation of the Hebrew Bible (39 Old Testament books), is produced. The 14 books of the Apocrypha are also included.

New Testament Era - AD (Anno Domini – The Year of our Lord)

45–100	Original 27 books of the Greek N.T. are written.
140-150	Marcion of Sinope's heretical "New Testament" prompted orthodox Christians to establish a New Testament canon, prompting the writings of the Creeds.
200	The Jewish Oral Torah, is first recorded.
240	Origen compiles the Hexapla, a six-columned parallel of Greek and Hebrew texts.
305-310	Lucian of Antioch's Greek New Testament text becomes the basis for the Textus Receptus.

312	Codex Vaticanus is possibly among the original 50 copies of the Bible ordered by Emperor Constantine. It is eventually kept in the Vatican Library in Rome.
367	Athanasius of Alexandria compiles the complete New Testament.
382-384	St. Jerome translates the New Testament from Greek into Latin. This latter becomes part of the Latin Vulgate manuscript.
390-405	St. Jerome translates the entire Bible from Greek into Latin.
500	Scriptures have been translated into over 500 languages.
600	The Roman Catholic Church declares Latin as the only language for Scripture.
680	Caedmon, English poet and monk translates the Bible and other books into Anglo Saxon poetry and song.
735	Bede, English historian, and monk, translates the Gospels into Anglo Saxon.
775	The Book of Kells, a richly decorated manuscript containing the Gospels and other writings, was completed by Celtic monks in Ireland.
865	Saints Cyril and Methodius begin translating the Bible into Old Church Slavonic.
950	The Lindisfarne Gospels manuscript is translated into Old English.
995-1010	Aelfric, an English abbot, translates parts of Scripture into Old English.

1205 Stephen Langton, theology professor and later Archbishop of Canterbury, created the first chapter divisions in the books of the Bible.

1229 The Council of Toulouse strictly forbids and prohibits lay people from owning a Bible.

1240 French Cardinal Hugh of Saint Cher published the first Latin Bible with the chapter divisions that still exist today.

1325 English hermit and poet, Richard Rolle de Hampole, and English poet William Shoreham translate the Psalms into metrical verse.

1330 Rabbi Solomon Ben Ismael first places chapter divisions in the margins of the Hebrew Bible.

1381-1382 John Wycliffe and associates, in defiance of the organized Church, believing that people should be permitted to read the Bible in their own language, began to translate and produce the first handwritten manuscripts of the entire Bible in English. These include the 39 Old Testament books, 27 New Testament books, and 14 Apocrypha books.

1388 John Purvey revises Wycliffe's Bible.

1415 - 31 years after Wycliffe's death, the Council of Constance charged him with more than 260 counts of heresy.

1428 - 44 Many years after Wycliffe's death, church officials dug up his bones, burned them, and scattered the ashes on Swift River.

1455   After the invention of the printing press in Germany, Johannes Gutenberg produced the first printed Bible, the Gutenberg Bible, in the Latin Vulgate.

The Reformation Era - The beginning of Protestantism and the widespread expansion of the Bible into human hands and hearts through printing and increased literacy.

1516   Desiderius Erasmus produces a Greek New Testament, a forerunner to the Textus Receptus.

1517   Daniel Bomberg's Rabbinic Bible contains the first printed Hebrew version (Masoretic text) with chapter divisions.

1522   Martin Luther translated and published the New Testament for the first time into German from the 1516 Erasmus version.

1524   Bomberg prints a second edition Masoretic text prepared by Jacob ben Chayim.

1525   William Tyndale produced the first translation of the New Testament from Greek into English.

1527   Erasmus publishes a fourth edition Greek-Latin translation.

1530   Jacques Lefèvre d'Étaples completes the first French-language translation of the entire Bible.

1535   Myles Coverdale's Bible completes Tyndale's work, producing the first complete printed Bible in the English language. It includes the 39 Old Testament books, 27 New Testament books, and 14 Apocrypha books.

1536 Martin Luther translates the Old Testament into the commonly-spoken dialect of the German people, completing his translation of the entire Bible in German.

1536 Tyndale is condemned as a heretic, strangled, and burned at the stake.

1537 The Matthew Bible (commonly known as the Matthew-Tyndale Bible), a second complete printed English translation, is published, combining the works of Tyndale, Coverdale, and John Rogers.

1539 The Great Bible, the first English Bible authorized for public use, is printed.

1546 Roman Catholic Council of Trent declares the Vulgate as the exclusive Latin authority for the Bible.

1553 Robert Estienne published a French Bible with chapter and verse divisions. This system of numbering has become widely accepted and is still found in most Bibles today.

1560 The Geneva Bible is printed in Geneva, Switzerland. It is translated by English refugees and published by John Calvin's brother-in-law, William Whittingham. The Geneva Bible is the first English Bible to add numbered verses to the chapters.

1568 The Bishop's Bible, a revision of the Great Bible, is introduced in England to compete with the popular but "inflammatory toward the institutional Church" Geneva Bible.

1582 Dropping its 1,000-year-old Latin-only policy, the Church of Rome produced the first English Catholic Bible, the Rheims New Testament, from the Latin Vulgate.

1592 The Clementine Vulgate (authorized by Pope Clementine VIII), a revised version of the Latin Vulgate, becomes the authoritative Bible of the Catholic Church.

1609 The Douay Old Testament is translated into English by the Church of Rome, to complete the combined Douay-Rheims Version.

1611 The KJV, also called the "Authorized Version" of the Bible is published. Over one billion copies in printed book to date.

1663 John Eliot's Algonquin Bible is the first Bible printed in America, not in English, but in the native Algonquin Indian language.

1782 Robert Aitken's Bible is the first English language (KJV) Bible printed in America.

1764 Anthony Purver publishers the Quaker Bible.

1790 Matthew Carey publishes a Roman Catholic Douay-Rheims Version English Bible in America.

1790 William Young prints the first pocket-sized "school edition" King James Version Bible in America.

1791 The Isaac Collins Bible, the first family Bible (KJV), is printed in USA.

1791 Isaiah Thomas prints the first illustrated Bible (KJV) in America.

1808 Jane Aitken, daughter of Robert Aitken is the first woman to print a Bible.

1808 Charles Thompson translated the Greek Septuagint and published the Thompson Bible.

1833 Noah Webster, after publishing his famous dictionary, released his own revised edition of the King James Bible.

1841 The English Hexapla New Testament, a comparison of the original Greek language and six important English translations is produced.

1844 The Codex Sinaiticus, a handwritten Koine Greek manuscript of both Old and New Testament texts dating back to the fourth century, is rediscovered by German Bible scholar Konstantin Von Tischendorf in the Monastery of Saint Catherine on Mount Sinai.

1862 Robert Young translated the Textus Receptus (The translation base for the first Greek translation of the N.T. into English by William Tyndale and is the textual base for the Bishops Bible, the Geneva Bible, and the King James Bible) and the Masoretic Text into the Youngs Literal Bible.

1881-1885 The King James Bible was revised and published as the Revised Version (RV) in England.

1883 Noah Webster published the Websters Revision and The Websters Dictionary.

1901 The American Standard Version, the first major American revision of the King James Version, is published.

1946-1952 The Revised Standard Version is published.

1947-1956 The Dead Sea Scrolls are discovered.

1960 New American Standard Bible the revision of the ASV is published.

BIBLE DOCTRINE

1960 King James Children's Version Bible is published.

1971 The New American Standard Bible (NASB) is published.

1973 The New International Version (NIV) is published.

1982 The New King James Version (NKJV) is published.

1986 The discovery of the Silver Scrolls, believed to be the oldest Bible text is found in the Old City of Jerusalem by Gabriel Barkay of Tel Aviv University.

1989 The New Revised Standard Version is published.

1996 The New Living Translation (NLT) is published.

1999 American King James Version is published.

2000 The World English Bible is published.

200   The English Standard Version (ESV) is published.

2004 The Holmans Bible is published.

2005 The New English Translation is published.

2011 The Modern English Version is published.

2017 The Christian Standard Bible is published.

Feed on the Word of God
and you will have a sure foundation for life.

BIBLE DOCTRINE

DOCTRINE OF CHURCH

The heart of God has always been to have a bride exclusive for Himself, and from the day Lucifer was cast out of Heaven, he opposed the plans of God against the Bride.

Genesis 3:15 The plan of Lucifer was a direct battle against Jesus, and this began in the garden of Eden.

In the Old Testament, the Bride was Israel and in the New Testament, the Bride is the Church.

This attack of the devil against the Bride has continued without pause throughout the Old Testament, but with the advent of the Incarnation and the birth (4 BC), Life, Crucifixion, Resurrection, and the Ascension of Christ, the intensity of the struggle just increased.

The first form of attack against the Church was to kill the believers.

Through the persecutions, the faith of the believers grew stronger, so the devil changed tactics against the Bride, by twisting the doctrine of the deity of Christ.

Then in AD 325, the devil moved against the doctrine of justification by faith.

In a final desperation the devil, knowing his time is short, came with another form of attack directly knocking the Bride with disunity and passivity.

There is a desperate need in the Church today for an equipping of the saints for the work of ministry, for the edifying of the Body of Christ, till we all come to the unity of the faith and the knowledge of the Son of God, to a perfect man, to the measure of the stature of the fullness of Christ.

In essence, the church needs a solid grounding and foundation of unity in faith, renewed identity, and ever-increasing deeper passion for the Presence of God.

The Word Church in Greek is Ekklesia and it is derived from the verb ekkaleo. The Verb is Ekkalieo is is made up of two words and they are;
- Ek means 'out'.
- Kaleo like kaleidoscope means to 'call or summon'.

Thus the literal meaning of the word church is 'to call out'.

The word synagogue in Greek is synagogue.

The word synagogue comes from a root word that means to gather.

The Church in Aramaic Old Testament is called Qahal and Edah.

Deuteronomy 9:10 On the day of the assembly ...

Deuteronomy 10:4 Then on the day of the assembly,...

Deuteronomy 23:3 No Ammonite or Moabite may enter the LORD'S assembly ...

The Aramain word Qahal and Edah is directly translated as The Church and it was called a Synagogue and the assembling together of God's people.
Genesis 28:3 May God Almighty bless you and make you fruitful and multiply you so that you become an assembly of peoples.

Leviticus 16:17 No one may be in the tent of meeting from the time he enters to make atonement in the most holy place until he leaves after he has made atonement for himself, his household, and the whole assembly of Israel.

The Synagogue (Qahal and Edah) was a place for sacred assembly.
Leviticus 23:3 ...but on the seventh day there must be a Sabbath of complete rest, a sacred assembly...

Qahal and Edah is found more than 150 times in the Pentateuch, while the word Ekklesia is mentioned almost 50 times in the New Testament.

The word church refers both to all believers, international Church which includes both the living and the dead, as well as to the individual local gatherings of believers called the local church.

BIBLE DOCTRINE

The Origin Of The Church:

The people of God began with Adam and Eve in the Garden of Eden. He created them in his image, which means that they are created in fellowship with their Maker. Genesis 3:16

Later, God called Abraham from a family of sun-worshippers and God entered into a covenant with him, promising to be His God, both to him and his descendants forever more. Genesis 17:7

Later God gave them David as king in Jerusalem. God promised to make David's descendants into a dynasty and to establish the throne of one of them forever.

2 Samuel 7:14-16 I will be a father to him, and he will be a son to Me. When he does wrong, I will discipline him with a human rod and with blows from others. But My faithful love will never leave him as I removed it from Saul; I removed him from your way. Your house and kingdom will endure before Me forever, and your throne will be established forever.'"

God then spoke to His chosen people through His prophets, and after they continually turned away from Him, God then pulled back for a period of 400 years until the last Old Testament prophet spoke of The Kingdom of God that was at Hand, then He, John the Baptist, went and baptized Jesus who became the Head of The church.

BIBLE DOCTRINE

The day of Pentecost marked the beginning of the New Testament Church.

Acts 1:5 On the day of Pentecost the Holy Spirit was poured out on the church and they (the Church) rose up in power.

Matthew 16:18 At the revelation with Peter seeing that Christ Is the son of the living God and Jesus himself turned around and said on this revelation in (Rock) I will build my Church.

Ephesians 2:20 The church is built on the foundation of the apostles and the prophets, as Christ Himself is the chief cornerstone

The church began with Adam and Eve in Genesis and from that time forward throughout the Old Testament God reinforced the foundation of the Church/Synagogue.

The foundation of the church was reinforced with Abraham in Genesis 12 and then again it was reinforced by John the Baptist in Matthew 3, ending the Old Testament and preparing the Way for the Church.
When Jesus started his ministry at the age of 30 years old, it was the final stages of the of the establishing and the New Testament Church.

When Jesus called his 12 apostles in Matthew 10, this was the first time the Church became a body with a head being Christ.

FOUNDATIONS OF FAITH

BIBLE DOCTRINE

In Matthew 16 When Peter made his confession of Who Christ is, then Christ made His first mention of the New Testament Church.

In Matthew 26 at the last supper, Jesus Christ instituted the ordinance of the Lord's Supper indicating that the church now existed.

In John 20:21,22 On the first Easter Sunday, the night after Jesus' resurrection He breathed on them and said to His disciples they must receive the Holy Ghost.

In Matthew 16 on the day of Pentecost, the New Testament Church was birthed and launched out to be Bride of Christ.

The Nature Of The Church.

The nature of the Church is like a family connected by faith through Jesus Christ., who is the head of the church.

The Church is built on the revelation of who Christ is.
Matthew 16:15-18 "But you," He asked them, "who do you say that I am?" Simon Peter answered, "You are the Messiah, the Son of the living God!" And Jesus responded, "Simon son of Jonah, you are blessed because flesh and blood did not reveal this to you, but My Father in heaven. And I also say to you that you are Peter, and on this rock I will build My church, and the forces of Hades will not overpower it.

The expansion growth of the church is through teachings and the wisdom of the New Testament apostles and prophets as well as the apostles and prophets in the present-day church, who minister to the local church as well as to the international church and submit to local Church leadership. In local churches, pastors their leadership carry the authority of local church leadership, while the five-fold ministry lays the foundation for maturity and church growth. The Ekklesia is not just a physical gathering; it's the invisible union of all believers across time. It's where believers join together, learning, growing, and supporting one another. These groups share the joy of worship, gain wisdom, and strengthen their faith through fellowship.

The Purpose Of The Church.

The Church exists to honor God above all else. It aims to glorify Him through a manifestation to the world, that we the Church are the image bearers of God.

The primary purpose for the church is to reflect His glory God in every situation and seek His Kingdom first.

Evangelism is so important, that Jesus Christ actually gave the Great Commission five times.

BIBLE DOCTRINE

Matthew 28:19 Go, therefore, and make disciples of all nations,

Mark 16:19 Go into all the world and preach the gospel to the whole creation.

Luke 24:47 You are witnesses of these things.

John 20:21 As the Father has sent Me, I also send you.

Acts 1:8 ... and you will be My witnesses in Jerusalem, in all Judea and Samaria, and to the ends of the earth.

The purposes of the Church are made manifest when five basic elements are put into daily practice:

1. Worship; Love the Lord with all your heart.
2. Ministry. Love your neighbor as yourself.
3. Evangelism. Go and make disciples.
4. Fellowship. Baptize them.
5. Discipleship. Equipping saints for works of service.

The discipleship factor of the purpose of the church is seen in the unity of the church, the maturity of the saints, and Kingdom expansion.

Kingdom of God expansion is the evangelism of the church and this has five elements to it.

1. Evangelism has the foundation.

2. Evangelism has the power.
3. Evangelism is the obligation.
4. Evangelism reaches all ethnic groups
5. Evangelism goes to the ends of the earth.

Ultimately, the Church's core is magnifying God's greatness.

The Attributes Of The Church.

The unity of the Church of Christ is profound and unmistakable. As highlighted in Ephesians 4:4-6, its unity is indivisible, embracing a singular body, Spirit, hope, Lord, faith, baptism, and God who reigns above all and within all. Who have their faith in found in Jesus Christ. This Church, designated as the "holy" nation in both Old Testament and the New Testament, comprises of individuals recognized as "saints" or "holy ones." Spanning both local denominations and international church which are one and the same, transcends barriers of age, race, language, nationality, and denomination.

Galatians 3:28 There is no Jew or Greek, slave or free, male or female; for you are all one in Christ Jesus.

The term "apostle," stemming from the Greek "apostolos," initially referred to a person commissioned or sent out. Its roots trace back to Phoenician origins, likened to an admiral leading a fleet. Romans later adapted it for appointing emissaries to expand their empire, a practice Jesus continued by conferring the title upon 27 individuals during His ministry. These apostles, coupled with prophets, form the bedrock of the Church, with Christ as its primary support and catalyst for growth, as elucidated in Ephesians 2:20 .. built on the foundation of apostles and prophets, with Christ Jesus Himself as the cornerstone.

While the Church remains apostolic, built on this foundation, its sustenance and ultimate fulfillment derive from Christ alone, not solely from apostles or prophets, as said in Hebrews 3:1-6 Therefore, holy brothers and companions in a heavenly calling, consider Jesus, the apostle and high priest of our confession; He was faithful to the One who appointed Him, just as Moses was in all God's household. For Jesus is considered worthy of more glory than Moses, just as the builder has more honor than the house. Now every house is built by someone, but the One who built everything is God. Moses was faithful as a servant in all God's household, as a testimony to what would be said in the future. But Christ was faithful as a Son over His household. And we are that household if we hold on to the courage and the confidence of our hope.

The Holy Spirit plays a vital role in unveiling Christ's teachings for the Church's edification, steering its course toward spiritual maturity and communal strength.

BIBLE DOCTRINE

The Marks Of A True Church.

The Church has one Lord, one faith, and one baptism. Ephesians 4:5,6 One Lord, one faith, one baptism, one God and Father of all, who is above all and through all and in all.

The Church is empowered by The Holy Spirit. Colossians 1:11 May you be strengthened with all power, according to His glorious might, for all endurance and patience, with joy

The Church practices holiness unto God. 1 Corinthians 1:2 To God's church at Corinth, to those who are sanctified in Christ Jesus and called as saints, with all those in every place who call on the name of Jesus Christ our Lord — both their Lord and ours.

The Church is one body in unity with many members, practicing one faith through a multi-diversity of cultures and tribes submitted to one another for The Glory of God. 1 John 1:1-4 What was from the beginning, what we have heard, what we have seen with our eyes, what we have observed and have touched with our hands, concerning the Word of life — that life was revealed, and we have seen it and we testify and declare to you the eternal life that was with the Father and was revealed to us — what we have seen and heard we also declare to you, so that you may have fellowship along with us; and indeed our fellowship is with the Father and with His Son Jesus Christ. We are writing these things so that our joy may be complete.

The Church practices the life-giving power of Communion. 1 Corinthians 10:16 The cup of blessing that we give thanks for, is it not a sharing in the blood of Christ? The bread that we break, is it not a sharing in the body of Christ?

The Church is a family with active fellowship with other saints and an active growing membership. Ephesians 4:12-16 In Him we have boldness and confident access through faith in Him. So then I ask you not to be discouraged over my afflictions on your behalf, for they are your glory. Prayer for Spiritual Power. For this reason, I kneel before the Father from whom every family in heaven and on earth is named. I pray that He may grant you, according to the riches of His glory, to be strengthened with power in the inner man through His Spirit,

The Church is devoted to sound biblical theology. 1 Timothy 1:5 Now the goal of our instruction is love that comes from a pure heart, a good conscience, and a sincere faith.

The Church is steadfast in obeying the apostles and prophets' doctrine. Ephesians 2:20 built on the foundation of the apostles and prophets, with Christ Jesus Himself as the cornerstone.

The Church practices winning the lost with evidence. Mark 1:15 The time is fulfilled, and the kingdom of God has come near. Repent and believe in the good news!

The Church practices active sending outreach ministries. Acts 13:3 Then after they had fasted, prayed, and laid hands on them, they sent them off.

The Church practices in reverence of The Lord. Hebrews 12:6 for the Lord disciplines the one He loves and punishes every son He receives.

The Church practices discipleship, equipping and sending. John 17:17 Sanctify them by the truth; Your word is truth.

The Church has servant leadership. Mark 10:42-44 You know that those who are regarded as rulers of the Gentiles dominate them, and their men of high positions exercise power over them. But it must not be like that among you. On the contrary, whoever wants to become great among you must be your servant, and whoever wants to be first among you must be a slave to all. For even the Son of Man did not come to be served, but to serve, and to give His life — a ransom for many.

The Church practices fervent prayer and intercession. Romans 10:1,2 Brothers, my heart's desire and prayer to God concerning them is for their salvation! I can testify about them that they have zeal for God, but not according to knowledge.

The Church practices speaking in tongues. 1 Corinthians 14:23 Therefore, if the whole church assembles together and all are speaking in other languages and people who are uninformed or unbelievers come in, will they not say that you are out of your minds?

The Church practices Divine healing and Divine health. James 5:16 Therefore, confess your sins to one another and pray for one another, so that you may be healed. The urgent request of a righteous person is very powerful in its effect.

The Church practices Anointed preaching. Luke 4:18 The Spirit of the Lord is on Me, because He has anointed Me to preach good news to the poor. He has sent Me to proclaim freedom to the captives and recovery of sight to the blind, to set free the oppressed,

The visible Church in the community. Acts 14:23 When they had appointed elders in every church and prayed with fasting, they committed them to the Lord in whom they had believed.

The invisible Church Philippians 3:20 but our citizenship is in heaven, from which we also eagerly wait for a Savior, the Lord Jesus Christ.

The Church And State Relationship.

The church and the state are both God-ordained institutions, under the law of God.

The church and the state are separate in their function and authority.

The state is subject to the authority of God, yet not subject to the authority of the church.

The State is a ministry of handling, obeying and enforcing God's governance in the country for the people.

The Church is a ministry of grace, obeying and enforcing the law of God in the preaching and teaching of the gospel of Jesus Christ.

The plan of God for the State is that God has given the State the power of the sword to enforce Christ's supremacy in civil matters.

God has given the church the power of the keys of the kingdom to enforce Christ's supremacy in spiritual and moral matters.

God's law is to be supreme in the state as well as in the church.

The Church is not to rule over the State and the State is not to rule over the Church.

God's law is to rule over both. Romans 13:1-7 Everyone must submit to the governing authorities, for there is no authority except from God, and those that exist are instituted by God. So then, the one who resists the authority is opposing God's command, and those who oppose it will bring judgment on themselves. For rulers are not a terror to good conduct, but to bad. Do you want to be unafraid of the authority? Do what is good, and you will have its approval. For government is God's servant for your good. But if you do wrong, be afraid, because it does not carry the sword for no reason. For government is God's servant, an avenger that brings wrath on the one who does wrong. Therefore, you must submit, not only because of wrath, but also because of your conscience. And for this reason you pay taxes, since the authorities are God's public servants, continually attending to these tasks. Pay your obligations to everyone: taxes to those you owe taxes, tolls to those you owe tolls, respect to those you owe respect, and honor to those you owe honor.

Leadership And Structure Of The Church.

Apart from the foundational offices of apostles and prophets, the early churches had leaders, who were chosen, called, and anointed into Church leadership according to Ephesians 4:11 'and he gave some, apostles; and some, prophets; and some, evangelists; and some, pastors and teachers.'

These ministry positions served the church under the Lordship of Jesus Christ, guided by both the Scripture and The Holy Spirit.

The offices of Church leadership and structure are not vertical or hierarchical in form or function, rather they are horizontal in structure and form of leadership, submitting one to one another and all submitting to Christ, while holding differing responsibilities with differing authority within the function of the given responsibility. The leadership authority was functional for the purpose of administration.

Christian Church leadership must never be confused with the counterfeit papal church leadership.

Christian Church leadership and function versus the Papal system (Roman Catholic Church) is vastly different.

The Christian Church Leadership originates in the book of Acts and is called to equip the saints for works of service while bringing the church to unity.

CHRISTIAN CHURCH	PAPAL SYSTEM –
Apostle governs, establishes government, and provides a foundation to build on.	Pope rules the Catholic Church in a very similar way to a king would a country, and he is the head of state for the Vatican City.
Prophets points the way and brings the vision of what God wants to build on that foundation	Cardinals are leading bishops and members of the College of Cardinals.
Evangelist gathers-outreach	Archbishop oversee large areas of churches called archdiocese.
Pastor guides or cares/nurturing for the sheep	Bishops are ministers who hold the full sacrament of holy orders.
Teacher grounds, or establishes the people in the word, raising Godly ministers	Priest: After graduating from being a Deacon, individuals become priests.
Deacons: workers in the church, that carry out forms of service for the gathering together (synagogue / church)	Deacons: Can practice in many similar ways to priests. They can baptize, witness marriages, and perform funerals.

international Church	Local Church / Ekklesia
Apostles	Pastor
Prophets	Elder
Teachers	Deacon – Workers in the church
Evangelists - Workers of miracles	Evangelists
Workers of healing	Administration
Ministry of helps	
Ministry of counseling	
Intercessors	

Apostles Mentioned In The New Testament:

People anointed to function in the office of an apostle were beyond the leadership structure of the twelve apostles called by Jesus at the beginning of His earthly ministry.:

1. The twelve Luke 9:1-6
2. The seventy Luke 10:1-10
3. Jesus Christ. Hebrews 3:1
4. Simon Peter. Matthew 10:2
5. Andrew. Matthew 10:2

6. James the son of Zebedee. Matthew 10:2
7. John. Matthew 10:2
8. Philip. Matthew 10:3
9. Bartholomew. Matthew 10:3
10. Thomas. Matthew 10:3
11. Matthew. Matthew. 10:3
12. James the son of Alphaeus. Matthew 10:3
13. Thaddaeus. Matthew 10:3
14. Judas the son of James. Luke 6:16
15. Simon the Zealot. Matthew 10:4
16. Judas Iscariot. Matthew 10:4
17. Matthias. Acts 1:26
18. Paul. Galatians 1:1
19. Barnabas. 1 Corinthians 9:5-6, Acts 14:4, 14
20. Andronicas. Romans 16:7
21. Junias. Romans 16:7
22. James, the Lord's brother. Galatians 1:19
23. Silas also called Silvanus. 1 Thess. 1:1, 2:6
24. Timothy. 1 Thessalonians 1:1, 2:6
25. Epaphroditus. Philippians 2:25
26. Apollos. 1 Corinthians 4:6-9 & 1 Corinthians 3:22
27. 1st of 2 Unnamed Apostles. 2 Corinthians 8:23
28. 2nd of 2 Unnamed Apostles. 2 Corinthians 8:23
29. Jude the Brother of Jesus is considered a possibility.

30. Mark – Author of Scripture.
31. Luke. Some early Church Fathers considered them to be apostles as they had authored Scripture.
32. The writer of Hebrews may have been an apostle as he authored scripture.
33. Titus. Similar in position and role to Timothy who was an apostle.

Leadership Structure In The Local Church / Ekklesia.

1. Elders, Overseers or Pastors. All three of these terms refer to the same function and were used interchangeably in the New Testament.
    a. 1 Peter 51,2 Elders, Overseers and Pastors are to shepherd the flock Church.
    b. These leaders were charged to lead, shepherd, teach, and equip the flock entrusted to them.
    c. The terms Elder and Overseer are two different titles that refer to the same office.
    d. The title of pastor is most commonly used today for the office that is designated to shepherd the Church, though it is used only one time in the New Testament. Ephesians 4:11
2. Elder: Episkopos – Acts 20:17

3. Overseer: Presbyteros - Acts 20:28
4. Pastor: Poimēn – Ephesians 4:11 is used only one time in the New Testament as a designation for a church leader.
5. Evangelist. The term evangelist is used only three times in the New Testament -
6. Teacher
7. Deacon, was intended to serve the needs of the flock and to enable the elders to carry out their responsibilities.

8. The Church leadership functions from the plurality of elders and not from the singular authority of one elder or pastor leading a congregation as the sole or primary leader.

The Plurality Of Elders In The Churches At:

1. The Church in Jerusalem. Acts 11:30 They did this, sending it to the elders by means of Barnabas and Saul.
2. The Churches in Antioch of Pisidia, Lystra, Iconium, and Derbe. Acts 14:23 When they had appointed elders in every church and prayed with fasting, they committed them to the Lord in whom they had believed.

3. The churches in Ephesus. 1 Timothy 5:17 The elders who are good leaders should be considered worthy of an ample honorarium, especially those who work hard at preaching and teaching.

4. The churches in Philippi. Philippians 1:1 Paul and Timothy, slaves of Christ Jesus: To all the saints in Christ Jesus who are in Philippi, including the overseers and deacons.

5. The churches in the cities of Crete. Titus 1:5 The reason I left you in Crete was to set right what was left undone and, as I directed you, to appoint elders in every town:

6. The churches to whom James wrote. James 5:14 Is anyone among you sick? He should call for the elders of the church, and they should pray over him after anointing him with olive oil in the name of the Lord.

7. The churches in the Roman provinces of Pontus, Galatia, Cappadocia, Asia, and Bithynia. ! Peter 5:1 Therefore, as a fellow elder and witness to the sufferings of the Messiah and also a participant in the glory about to be revealed, I exhort the elders among you:

The Authority Of Elders

Elders, Overseers and Pastors possess authority in the local Church. Starting from the Apostolic age in AD30, throughout the medieval ages, and up to the present day, churches, seminaries and monasteries have been started by founding fathers of the church called Elders, Overseers and Pastors.

Paul instructs the Thessalonian Church to respect those who "labor" among them, who "are over you. 1 Thessalonians 5:12 Now we ask you, brothers, to give recognition to those who labor among you and lead you in the Lord and admonish you,

The Church is called to obey and submit to Elders, Overseers and Pastors. Hebrews 13:17 Obey your leaders and submit to them, for they keep watch over your souls as those who will give an account, so that they can do this with joy and not with grief, for that would be unprofitable for you. As shepherds, Elders, Overseers, and Pastors are given the task to guard the Local Church. Acts 20:28 Be on guard for yourselves and for all the flock that the Holy Spirit has appointed you to as overseers, to shepherd the church of God, which He purchased with His own blood.

As representatives, Elders, Overseers and Pastors speak and act on behalf of the entire congregation. Acts 20:17 Now from Miletus, he sent to Ephesus and called for the elders of the church.

The authority of the Elders, Overseers and Pastors comes from God and not an electoral committee. Acts 20:28 Be on guard for yourselves and for all the flock that the Holy Spirit has appointed you to as overseers, to shepherd the church of God, which He purchased with His own blood.

The authority of Elders, Overseers and Pastors is never absolute. Galatians 1:8 But even if we or an angel from heaven should preach to you a gospel other than what we have preached to you, a curse be on him!

Pastors should submit to the Elders and Overseers of the local Church for all decision making, yet the final authority the Pastor is the called set person who carries responsibility.

The authority that the Elders, Overseers and Pastors possess is not so much found in their office, but rather in the duties they perform.

The qualifications & duties of Elders, Overseers and Pastors:

There is no official record for the qualifications of a Pastor.
As stated earlier, the word Elders, Overseers or Pastors refer to the same function and were used interchangeably in the New Testament.

It can be confidently stated that the qualifications and duties for Elders and Overseers would apply to Pastors. 1 Timothy 3:1-7 This saying is trustworthy: "If anyone aspires to be an overseer, he desires a noble work." An overseer, therefore, must be above reproach, the husband of one wife, self-controlled, sensible, respectable, hospitable, an able teacher, not addicted to wine, not a bully but gentle, not quarrelsome, not greedy — one who manages his own household competently, having his children under control with all dignity. (If anyone does not know how to manage his own household, how will he take care of God's church?) He must not be a new convert, or he might become conceited and fall into the condemnation of the Devil. Furthermore, he must have a good reputation among outsiders, so that he does not fall into disgrace and the Devil's trap.

The qualifications and duties should represent the characteristics for all believers.

The qualifications and duties for a Believer, Leader, Elder or Pastor is not on the function of responsibility, but rather on who the person is and their personal testimony.

The only qualification that directly relates to the duties in the Church of Leader, Elder or Pastor, is that he must be "able to teach. 1 Timothy 3:2 An overseer, therefore, must be above reproach, the husband of one wife, self-controlled, sensible, respectable, hospitable, an able teacher.

Ten Requirements To Function As A Leader, Elder Or Pastor:

1. The calling is from God.
2. The anointing of the Holy Spirit to function in the position.
3. The appointing from God into the position.
4. A teachable, humble heart.
5. A passion to see the lost saved.
6. A genuine heart of an intercessor.
7. An increasing passion to honor God through worship.
8. A Kingdom of God heart and not a self-made kingdom.
9. A true equipper of the saints in the local Church.
10. The family lifestyle of the Leader, Elder or Pastor is honorable, without reproach.

The Office Of Deacon

The word "deacon" comes from the Greek term diakonos which means servant.

The title deacon has 29 occurrences in the New Testament and 3 times does deacon refer to an office-holder.

Romans 16:1 I commend to you our sister Phoebe, who is a servant of the church in Cenchreae.

Philippian 1:1 Paul and Timothy, slaves of Christ Jesus:
To all the saints in Christ Jesus who are in Philippi, including the overseers and deacons.

1 Timothy 3:8 Deacons, likewise, should be worthy of respect, not hypocritical, not drinking a lot of wine, not greedy for money,

Deacons are not required to teach. 1 Timothy 3:2 An overseer, therefore, must be above reproach, the husband of one wife, self-controlled, sensible, respectable, hospitable, an able teacher,

Deacons do not rule or lead the congregation but have a service heart ministry.

Both Leader, Elder or Pastor and Deacons must lead their families well.
The Apostle Paul does include the deacons, where he compares managing one's household to taking care of God's church. 1 Timothy 3:5 If anyone does not know how to manage his own household, how will he take care of God's church?

The ministry function of deacon is most important in the church for the daily operations.

Six Present-day functions of leadership and structure for the local Church should be:

1. The senior Leader, Elder or Pastor (possibly husband and wife team) who carry the calling and anointing function in as lead Leader, Elder or Pastor.
   This position and function flow from a horizontal form of servant leader.
2. A general board of God anointed Leaders, Elders or Pastors who stand in support and counsel for the senior Leader, Elder or Pastor.
   This position and function flow from a horizontal form of leadership hold the senior Leader, Elder or Pastor accountable and supporting joint decisions.
3. A general executive committee who are elected for a season and comprising of a secretary, treasurer and overseer.
4. Deacons and helpers who are chosen by the Leaders, Elders and Pastors to serve in various capacities.
5. Church members and congregants of the local church vote actions and functions and nomination of deacon positions.
6. Church membership is founded on the applicants personal work with God as good standing testimony and their spiritual commitment and loyalty to the local Church.

BIBLE DOCTRINE

Church History Time Line:

Matthew 16:18 Jesus said, "I will build My Church and the gates of hell will not prevail against it."

And in Matthew 28:19 'Go, therefore, and make disciples of all nations,'

The direct translation in Greek is, 'matheteusate panta ta ethna', and the translation for this is, "make disciples of all ethnic groups,"

Growth is inevitable when Jesus builds. Even with the onslaught of extreme persecution, and direct attack against doctrine, the church grew from strength to strength.

The church has been built, and is still being built on the Apostles and Prophets doctrine dating from the first church plant in the book of Acts throughout the medieval ages through monastic era, and up till the present-day church, God has used men and women who are called apostles, prophets, overseers, elders, pastors and other ministries for the Kingdom of God expansion and church growth.

The gates of hell cannot stand against us, as we have a proven track-record throughout history, that the churches thrived the most under persecution.

This is visibly seen in China under the hardliners of the communist party against any form of religious faith, especially that of Christianity.

In China, this meant the confiscation of all Bibles and Christian literature. The Stifling and the remaining of institutionalized Christianity. The closure of all church buildings. Public humiliation of Christians through physical and emotional assault. Emotional and physical persecution, and most times ending in martyrdom.

Imprisonment and hard labor with the purpose of cracking the person into denying their faith in the labor camps, the labor factories, and the work farms.

This extreme persecution and martyrdom has caused the church to flourish under pressure, like crushed olives producing pure oil.

Below is a brief overview of New Testament church in history showing the growth from its New Testament birthing in AD 30 to the present day.

4? BC Marks the birth of Jesus in Bethlehem of Judea.

29 Jesus begins His public ministry at the age of 30 with signs, wonders and miracles, after his baptism by John and during the rule of Pilate.

29 In the 15yr. of Tiberius rule, John started his ministry and preached, Repent, for the kingdom of heaven is near' Matthew 3:1-2c

30–100 The Apostolic Age of the Church, and the original 27 books of the Greek N.T. are written.

33 Jesus is crucified, buried and resurrected, then appears to more than 500 disciples at one time. 1 Corinthians 15:6

Jesus gives the great commission. Matthew 28:19

After 40 days Jesus ascends into Heaven. Acts 1:3,9

33   Sivan 6 (May-June) The founding members of the New Testament was 120 Jews and Jewish Proselytes on the day of Pentecost.

52   Thomas goes to India to plant churches.

58   The first Churches were planted in Jerusalem and from there onward multiplied and planted into Illyricum, into Syria, Asia Minor, Greece, Italy, Jerusalem, Antioch, and Rome. Ephesus, Corinth, Samaria, Damascus, Joppa, Caesarea, Tyre and Cyprus. Including the provinces of Asia Minor, Troas, Philippi, Thessalonica, Berea, Athens, Crete, Patmos, Malta, Puteoli and then onto Ethiopia.

The Apostolic Fathers, Bishops and Overseers of the Church who invariably planted and led churches.

A.D. 98 – A.D. 590

98   Clement of Rome.

110   Ignatius of Antioch.

155   Tertullian. Bishop and apologist, a defender of doctrine.

165   Justin Matyr. Bishop and apologist, a defender of doctrine.

167   Polycarp.

167   Didache.

167   Barnabus.

167   Shepherd of Hermas.

180   Tatien. (Bishop and apologist, a defender of doctrine.)

202   Irenaeus.

216   Clement of Alexandria.

220   Tertullian wrote of a strong Christian community in Persia.

251   OriGenesis (One of the most distinguished Church Fathers)

258   Cyprian the Bishop of Carthage in North Africa.

325-590   Huge changes occurred both in the church and in the political arena. The western Roman Empire collapsed under the assaults of German Barbarian Tribes and Roman Catholicism was birthed.

The Christian Church stayed true to the statutes and principals of Creeds that had been established under the Elders, Overseers (Bishops) and Pastors throughout the Medieval Church and Scholasticism era (590-1517)

339   Eusebius of Caesarea. (Known as the father of Church history). Bishop Eusebius was the counselor and advisor to Constantine the Great, who was famed for the Edict of Milan in 313 that legalized and legitimized Christianity in the Roman Empire for the first time. Constantine was the first Christian Roman Emperor. His mother and other family members were also believers who contributed to his actions to propagate the Gospel.

367 Bishop Epiphanius of CyprIsaiah

370 Basil the Great, Bishop of Cappadocia.

373 Athanasius, was Bishop of Alexandria and wrote a treatise on the Incarnation, affirming and explaining that Jesus was both God and Man. He was the first person to identify the 27 books of the New Testament. The Athanasian Creed is ascribed to Bishop Athanasius.

380	The birth of Roman Catholic church under the rule Emperor Theodosius who issued the edict of Thesolonica of Roman Catholic church becomes the official State church.
397	Bishop of Milan, the fighter of heresy.
430	Augustine the Bishop of Hippo was the equivalent to Apostle Paul.
432	Bishop Patrick of Ireland preached and planted churches with a great Christian awakening of almost the entire nation.
450	Bishop Eutyches was Shepherd over the Churches in Constantinople.
455	Prosper Aquitanus continued as Pastor/Overseer from Augustine of Hippo in South Western France.
484-519	The first of the schisms called the Acacian schism between the eastern Church and western Church.

The Eastern Church (Greek) believed in Miaphysitism. That is to believe that Jesus is the Incarnate Word of God and is 100% Divine and yet fully 100 % human.

The Western Church (Latin) believed in Zenoism also known as Henotikonism. That is believing the Emperor of Rome is all divine. |
| 491 | The Armenian Church split from East and West churches. The Armenian Church was birthed from one the mission trips of Apostle Bartholomew who was mostly a Church planter in India. A.D. 30- A.D.65 |
| 496 | King of the Francs. Clovis 1st is baptized and opens the doors for France and Church growth. |

BIBLE DOCTRINE

498-506 The Anti-Pope schism that started with Laurentius of Santa Prassede who spoke against heresies of the papal church.

The Medieval Church and Scholastic Era

1517-1590

This period of was dominated by the Roman Catholic Church, which is the papal church and the counterfeit church to the true Bride of Christ.

1. The Crusades. 1097-1244

    1097-1099   1st crusade and more than 70,000 march to the Holy Land and on route slaughter Jews in Germany and pillage their villages to cover costs.

    1146   2nd crusade with tens of thousands killed and a total fail.

    1189-1192   3rd crusade Richard the Lion Heart negotiates access to Jerusalem for Christians and Jews.

    1202   4th crusade to defeat Egypt resulting with a divination between the eastern and western churches.

    1208 5th crusade against the Albigensians with the destruction of Church growth.

    1212 6th crusade using children and the slaughter of tens of thousands of children.

    1217 7th crusade fails against Egypt with further church destruction.

    1229   8th crusade recovers Jerusalem through negotiations.

    1244   Muslims recapture Jerusalem by force with many killed.

2. The Great Schism. 1378-1348

3. The Inquisition. 1184-1230
4. The dominance of the Roman Catholic Church. 380-to present.

Throughout this difficult time of known as the dark ages, God still had church planters called Bishops, Elders, Overseers and Pastors who also planted Churches, established training centers, Christian seminaries and monasteries. This period in history is known as the monastic era. Monasticism was a founded on the lifestyle and identification to a Christ centered lifestyle of severe self-discipline and avoidance of all forms of indulgence to denying the world with purpose to seeking to know God and the study of His Word.

529   Bishop Benedict of Nursia of Italy founded 12 Christian Seminaries / Monasteries.

530   Bishop Benedict of Nursia of Italy founded Christian Seminary / Monastery of Monte Cassino.

543   Bishop Origen, (A Church Father) the most anointed writer of the early Church, having written over 2000 thesIsaiah Emperor Justinian condemned Bishop Origen as a heretic. The Word of God says, 'touch not My anointed and do my prophets no harm.' World disasters took place after Emperor Justinian condemned Bishop OriGenesis

   1. This season was known as 'dendrochronilogical disaster era' worst natural disaster era in world history.

2. Justinian's plague (Yersinia pestis – black rat plague) claiming the lives of millions of people arriving in Constantinople sweeping throughout the Mediterranean and lasted for over 225 years.

3. Multi volcanic eruptions, tsunamis and droughts worldwide.

550 Bishop David of Mynyw from Wales plants Churches across Wales and births revival.

563 Columba a Bishop of Ireland birthed the Hiberno-Scottish mission.

567 Bishop Magnus Aurelius Cassiodorus Senator started a Seminary/Monastery in Vivarium and Mantecastello.

590-604 Pope Gregory the Great is considered the greatest pope ever that truly did value to the Christian Church, established the Gregorian Chant which is the confessing of the 7 deadly things that God hates: Lust, Gluttony, Greed, Sloth, Wrath, Envy, Pride.

596 Bishop Augustine, the Apostle to the English and founder of the Old English Church.

600 Bishop Evagrius Scholasticus, father of Church/Ecclesiastical History.

612 The Seminary / Monastery of Bobbio in Northern Italy is established.

613 Bishop Gall established the Seminary / Monastery of St Gallen in Switzerland.

614 Bishop Pacidus and Bishop Sigisbert founded the Seminary / Monastery called the Disentis Abbey in Canton of Graubunden in eastern Switzerland.

624	The rise of the Islam empire and their 1st battle (6yrs) against other Arabic tribes making them the dominant people. The children of Hagar become the thorn in the flesh against Israel and the rest of the world.
625	Bishop Paulinus, a church planter was born an Italian and went to Northumbria, England. He was known to be prophetic in action as and evangelist leading many to salvation.
628	Bishop Bibai the Great, father of the Church in Asia and church planter in the East passes away.
634	Umar, the 2nd Suni leader Islam invades Syria, closes and destroys many Churches.
718	Arch Bishop Boniface, the planter of many churches to the Germans.
731	Bede The Monk who wrote on English Church History was also a Church planter in England.
781	Xi'an Stele, 150 documents on a block of limestone showing early Christian mission and Church planting in China.
849	Bishop Ansgar was the Apostle of the Northern Europe including Denmark and Sweden.
863	The two brothers, Cyril and Methoius both Apostles and Bishops to the Slavs planted many churches and revivals.
966	The Duke of Poland, Mieszko the 1st. becomes a believer and opens the door for Poland to serve God and many churches are planted.

988   Eastern Europe (The Hus) opens to the Gospel and Hungary has many Christian churches planted there.

AD 1000

1054   The great Schism and main schism of division between the Roman catholic church and Christian Church was over the pope being the head of the total church and the eucharist being the full body and flesh of Jesus and the wine being the true blood. This disagreement officiated the disunity of the papal church and B ride of Christ.

1065   The Seminary / Monastery / Abbey / Church (West Minster Abbey) built under the influence of the Bishop Benedict from A.D.529

1079   Stanislaus, Bishop of Poland planted Churches and was used to raise people from the dead was latter executed.

1082   Abbot Count Conrad of Stellenburen of Adelheim built the Abby (Church) of Engelberg.

1097   Over 70,000 march in the 1st crusade to take back the Holy Land. On route they slaughter many Jews in Germany and pillage their villages to cover costs and at the same time build castles and church buildings.

AD 1100

1124   Pomerania converted from Slavic paganism to Christianity and planted six monasteries / Seminary training centers and churches.

1128 David of Scotland found the Church of Holyrood in Edinburgh Scotland. This was the church for all local until it was destroyed in the 18th century.

1131 Peter of Bruys the Teacher of Truth was burned at the stake

1131 Walter de Clare from Normandy, founded Tintern Abbey (Church), Wales.

1100-1200 the Petrobrusians rejected infant baptism.

1170 Peter Valdes Waldo a wealthy man from Lyons, France gave his wealth to the poor and becomes an itinerant preacher. He valued poverty as the basis for Christian life and the necessity for all Christians to preach the gospel and started the Waldensians movement.

1146 2nd crusade with tens of thousands killed and a total fail.

1189-1192 3rd crusade Richard the Lion Heart negotiates access to Jerusalem for Christians and Jews.

1190 Christianity spreads to Finland and many churches are established.

AD 1200

1209 Francis of Assisi gives away his wealth and starts evangelism outreach and itinerant preaching, called the Franciscans.

1211 The Church of Mongolia rises in strength under the influence of Genghis Khan's mother (Hoelun).

1217 Francis of Asissi preaches to the Sultan.

1269 Kublai Kahn requested from Marco Polo and his Italian merchant family called the Polos family to send 100 teachers of religion to instruct the Chinese in the learning and faith of Europe. Only two Dominican Friars went and on route they gave up returned back to Europe. (This was known to be the greatest fail in church history for Church growth.)

AD 1300

1302 Fransicans plant many churches throughout Mongolia.

1326 Metropolitan Peter preachers and planted churches from Kiev to Moscow.

1337 Sergii Radonezhskii starts a church small wooded church in Russia and grows it into a seminary and monastery called Troitse-Sergiyeva Lavra.

1342 Marsilius of Padua was a Doctor, Preacher and Bishop at the University of ParIsaiah

1348-1351 The pubonic kills 33% of Europen population. (+/- 40 million)

1371 John Wycliffe challenges Roman Catholicism.

1382 John Wycliffe translates the Bible into English for all to read.

AD 1400

1411 John Huss was a synodical preacher and Bishop.

1415 John Wycliff translated the Bible

1431 Joan of Arc is burned at the stake

1452 Official decree from the Roman Catholic church sanctioning salve trade from West Africa to Europe.

1455 The Gutenberg Bible is first printed by Johan Gutenberg.

AD 1500

1500 Willian Tyndale translated the Bible into English and was local church pastor in England.

1517 Martin Luther posts his 95 thesis and birthing of the protestant reformation and served as Pastor and confessor at Castle Church and All Saints Church.

1525 The beginning of the Anabaptist movement.

1552 Bishop Francis Xavier from Spain preached on Shanguan Island China performing many miracles and planting churches.

1536-1564 John Calvin was the father of the theological system and helped lead in the Church of Geneva.

1563 Theodore Beza, a successor to John Calvin was Bishop to the Pastors, Leaders and Elders in Geneva and throughout France.

1533 Thomas Cranmore becomes Archbishop Canterbury and 1538 was burned at the stake.

1547 John Knox started preaching during the reign of bloody queen Mary and then went to Frankfurt Germany to be a pastor.

1603 Yi Gwangj-Jeong, a Korean diplomat travelled to Beijing and on his return to Korea he carried several theological books written by Matteo Ricci, an Italian Jesuit missionary and church into China.

1647 George Fox preached and was the key figure in the quakers movement.

The Enlightenment Church (1648–1789)

Churches were planted across the world during this season. This was a time when man began to cast off the superstition and fear of the medieval world. The effort to seek the Lord, led to the discovery of natural laws which governed the universe and led to scientific, political and social advances. Enlightenment thinkers examined the rational basis of all beliefs and in the process rejected the authority of roman catholic church and state.

1650 John Owen one of the greatest theologians of the English Puritan movement and was known to be the true pastor of pastors.

1716 Jonathan Edwards at the age of 13 yrs old graduated from Yale and at the age of 16 yrs old received his masters of divinity. He became the Pastor and was the most significant American pastor of the 18th century.

1738 George Whitefiled was a Bishop over many churches and an international preacher.

1735 Howell Harris from Wales was a Bishop and one of the key leaders of the Welsh Methodist revival.

1735 John Wesley and his brother Charles went to the America as missionaries to the native Americans and planted churches. Later he returned to England and was inspired by the Great Awakening in New England, he became an international revivalist throughout UK. He rode his horses over 250,000 miles and preached over 42000 sermons and planted numerous churches.

1740 Charles Wesley was a prophetic worshiper who wrote numerous hymns.

1758 Angus Toplady a prophetic worshiper wrote Rock of Ages cleft for me .... He raised the standard of worship in the church.

1758 King Yeonjo from Korea officially outlawed Catholicism.

The Modern Church (1798–1970)

1790 Friedrich Scheiermacher was the father of modern theology and a reformed pastor.

1790 Yi Seung-hun preached and baptized people across Korea, he martyred the same year.

1795 A Chinese Pastor Kang was smuggled into Korea and planted underground churches.

1795 - Sister Kang Wan-suk (Columba), a wealthy aristocratic woman, protected and hid the Pastor Kim Beom. Sister Kang was tortured and beheaded.

1801 Caneridge Revival of Kentucky causing huge church growth.

1845 The first Korean priest, Kim Dae-geon (Andrew), was ordained. He was discovered with a Korean bible and he was executed.

1880 The Missionary Awakening

1828 Plymouth brethren was founded and planted many churches.

1830 Charles Finney revival meetings lead to 2nd great awakening in America.

1842 David Livingstone preaches across Africa and plants many churches.

1844 Hans Paludan Smith Schreuder is missionary and arrives in Natal, South Africa and plans churches.

1847 John Christian Frederick Heyer a missionary, arrives in Andhra Pradesh, India

1851 Charles Spurgeon preached his first message at the age of 16yrs old. He was a Pastor of New Park Street Chapel in Southwark, Bishop and Christian theologian. He frequently preached to crowds of over 10,000 people. He had what was known as the first mega-church.

Dwight L. Moody founded the Northfield School of Theology, the Moody Church and the Moody Bible Institute in Chicago.

1857 The Prayer Revival started opening the doors for worldwide church revival.

1854 Hudson Taylor arrives in China and plants 100's of churches.

1859 Ashbel Green Simonton a missionary, arrives in Brazil and founds Presbyterian Church of Brazil, the oldest Brazilian Protestant denomination.

1865 William Booth founds the Salvation Army, vowing to bring the gospel into the streets to the most desperate and needy

1866 8,000 Christians and Catholics are executed in Korea.

1865 Dr. Robert Morrison - comes to Korea He came from Chefoo in China on an old American navy merchant ship 'SS General Sherman'. There were twenty-one people on board the SS Sherman, including Robert Jermain Thomas. The ship sailed up the Taedong River and Robert Jermain Thomas gave away 500 Bibles. When they approached Pyongyang, the chief of police Lee Hyon Ik boarded the ship and the crew took him hostage and held him captive, hoping to persuade the Koreans to give them food and safe passage in return for his release. The Koreans managed to seize back the hostage A fight against the sailor and Korean police took place and on both sides, people were killed. The Koreans set fire to the ship. Most of the passengers and crew escaped the fire, but were killed by Korean soldiers when they reached the shore. Thomas opened up his case of Bibles and was throwing them onto the shore, shouting 'Jesus, Jesus'. Then, after some time, with his clothes on fire he jumped overboard clutching a number of Bibles. He was seized on the shore by soldiers. Thomas gave a Bible to the soldier who captured him – Choon Kwon Park. Thomas was 27 yrs old and was taken before the governor, and gave his last Bible to his executioner. He knelt and prayed before being beheaded. Later, his body, along with the others, was buried on an island in the middle of the river, the spot where Thomas Memorial Church was built 1932.

1870 Ŭiju - near the modern-day border between North Korea and China. Several young Koreans business men met John Ross and John McIntyre, two Presbyterian missionaries. The Korean business men taught the missionaries the Korean language and helped them translate the Chinese Bible into in Korean Language. The Korean men were baptized and returned to Ŭiju and started a church there.

1880 Suh Sang-ryun (1848–1926) Sorae, Suh carried copies of a Korean translation of the Gospel of Luke there and began to pastor a group of Korean believers.

1881 Missionaries arrives in New Guinea

1885 First Western missionaries - Horace Grant Underwood and Henry Gerhard from the USA arrive in Korea.

1886 Johan Fliérl a missionary, arrives in New Guinea and plants many churches.

1890 Samuel A. Moffett arrives in Pyongyang Korea and plants many churches.

1899 Mrs. Kim Gang planted churches and preached about the emancipation of women from the bondage of thousands of years.

1899 Gideons International Inter-national was founded Open Doors for the Bible to get into many closed countries.

1903 First group baptism at Sattelberg Mission Station under Christian Keyser in New Guinea paves way for mass conversions during the following years.

1903 - Wonsan Revival Wonsan, with many thousands being born again and many churches being birthed.

1904 Welsh revival and the birth of many churches.

1907–1910 The Pyongyang Revival with many 1000's coming to Christ and many churches planted.

An old man named Chu Won Park went confessed publicly that he had been the one who had killed Thomas, nearly 40 years before. The impact of this testimony on the meeting was profound. This old man's son eventually became an elder of the Presbyterian Church in Korea.

1906–1909 The Azusa Street Revival in Los Angeles California begins modern Pentecostal movement and birthing 1000's of churches worldwide.

1917 True Jesus Church was founded in Beijing

1923-1955 David A. McGavran, missionary to India, sent out by United Christian Missionary Society, is recognized as the Grandfather of the modern Church Growth Movement.

1926 Wathman Nee established the Christian Assemblies known as the Little Flock in China.

1929 Through the East African Revival many churches are started.

1930 Revival breaks out in Shungtung China and churches are planted.

1947 Oral Roberts founded Evangelistic Association of churches and leaders.

1947 Dead sea scrolls are discovered.

1948 WCC (World Council of Churches) is the false Ekklesia.

1948 The declaration and establishment of the State of Israel.

1949 Billy Graham preaches his first crusade in Los Angeles and the church grows.

1951 Campus Crusade is founded, resulting in the planting of many churches.

1954 The founding of the Three Self-Patriotic Movement (TSPM) fake church of China.

1954 The founding of the house church movement in China growing at today an estimated of 10 million churches with 50 million members.

1960-1980 Conversion Boom

1960 The Word of faith movement begins and churches grow.

1963 Oral Roberts University was founded sending 1000's of missionaries across the world and planting 1000's of churches worldwide.

1970 The Jesus movement takes hold in the U.S. and many churches are planted.

1971 The Jesus Movement begins.

1973 Trinity broadcasting network was founded by Jan and Paul Crouch encouraging and building into many churches.

1974 Jim Bakker founded PTL television ministry encouraging and building into many churches.

1977 Focus on the Founded was founded by Dr. Dobson.

1980 The Vineyard movement supporting and planting churches around the world.

2020 House church expansion throughout the world, especially in India, Egypt and the Middle East.

Post 2020 – present-day. Social media has helped tremendously in the Word of God being preached across the world.

The church has exploded in growth under pressure with the outpouring of the Holy Spirit, and the promise of God that God will build his house in the gates of hell will not prevail against it.

We have seen, and we can see the growth being exponential in every area of life, and in every society.

BIBLE DOCTRINE

DOCTRINE OF MAN

The doctrine of man is also called anthropology and the definition of Anthropology is the study of man, humanity or a person.

The word anthropology is derived from anthropos and logia.

In Greek Anthropos is the study of man, humanity, humankind, or person.

In Greek Logia is the knowledge or study of.

To study the doctrine of man outside of the written word of God, is futile and always leads to death, as the ways that seem right to a man, leads to death. Job 14:12

It is impossible for the mind of carnal man to find true illumination of his identity outside revelation given by the Spirit of God. Although man may think it wise in pursuing truth through the human reason and intellect, without the counsel of Divine wisdom and the acknowledgment and acceptance of God's truth, mankind end up questioning the very essence of truth.

Isaiah 55:8,9 For My thoughts are not your thoughts, and your ways are not My ways." This is the LORD'S declaration. "For as heaven is higher than earth, so My ways are higher than your ways, and My thoughts than your thoughts.

John 18:38 What is truth?" said Pilate.

Proverbs 14:12 There is a way that seems right to a man, but its end is the way to death.

Psalms 8:4 what is man that You are thinking of him, ...

Genesis 1:26 Then God said, "Let Us make man in Our image, according to Our likeness. ...

In essence, man is a little god, created in the image and likeness of YAHWEH.

Psalms 82:6 I said, "You are gods; you are all sons of the Most High.

John 10:34 Jesus answered them, "Isn't it written in your scripture, I said, you are gods?

The Trinity Of Mankind.

Like the Trinity that has three distinct members, The Father, The Son and The Holy Spirit, so man too is a trinity with three distinct parts consisting of a body, a soul, and a spirit.

1 Thessalonians 5:23 Now may the God of peace Himself sanctify you completely. May your spirit, soul, and body be kept sound and blameless for the coming of our Lord Jesus Christ.

1. The Body of Man.

The body of man is flesh, bone, and blood which were made from the dust. It is identified by the five senses, sight, (eyes) hearing, (ears) smelling, (nose) talking, (mouth) touch. The body has no power of its own to decide what to do or not, it only carries out the instruction received from inside.

Genesis 2:7 Then the LORD God formed the man out of the dust from the ground and breathed the breath of life into his nostrils, and the man became a living being.

Only at the moment of death does the soul separate from the flesh the fleshly corpse returns to the dust of the Earth and the immortal soul, which is spirit, passes into eternity.

Genesis 2:7, 3:19 You will eat bread by the sweat of your brow until you return to the ground, since you were taken from it. For you are dust, and you will return to dust."

This explains why the body will not be judged by God.
Ecclesiastes 12:7 and the dust returns to the earth as it once was,
and the spirit returns to God who gave it.

The nature of man's spirit at the moment of physical death (holy or unholy) determines the soul's final abode. That departed soul still retains a recognizable bodily form complete with members like eyes and a tongue and is cognizant of being and can experience sensations

Luke 16:24 Father Abraham!' he called out, 'Have mercy on me and send Lazarus to dip the tip of his finger in water and cool my tongue, because I am in agony in this flame!'

2. The Soul of Man.

The soul of man becomes a living soul at conception, which is born into sin, though at the point of conception until the age of accountability is not judged for personal sin as the child is not conscious of conscious of sin. At the age of accountability the soul of man falls from Grace into being accountable for the personal consequence of personal sin, and only through salvation is the judgment of sin removed from the person.

The soul is the part of man between the body and the spirit, yet it is not a mixture of two. The soul is made up three of parts being the mind, will, and emotions which work through perception, interception, proprioception, and vestibular.

SENSES	Carnal man	Surrendered	Demonic
Perception, interoception, proprioception and vestibular	Acts 17:28 In Him, you live and have your being.	Psalms 139:13 You created my inward parts…	Mark 8:17 Do you not perceive?
Mind	Colossians 3:2 Set your mind on things above …	Ephesians 4:23 Be renewed in the your mind…	Ephesians 2:1-3 Desires of the mind…
Will	Romans 9:16 not on the human will…	John 4:34 Do the will of Him who sent you?	Leviticus 20:6 Person who turns to mediums
Emotions	Ecclesiastes 3:4 Time to weep, time to laugh, time to mourn, a time to dance…	Joshua 1:9 do not be frightened, do not be dismayed…	1 Samuel 16:14 Distressing spirit

3. The Spirit of Man.

Proverbs 20:27 The spirit of man is the lamp of Jehovah, searching all his innermost parts.

The spirit of man is life from God, and this means that without your spirit you would be dead.

James 2:26 For as the body apart from the spirit is dead, even so faith apart from works is dead.

Ecclesiastes 8:8 No one has power over the spirit to retain the spirit, and no one has power in the day of death.

Therefore, the spirit of man is life from God and is also connected with breath of God.

Genesis 2:7 And the LORD God formed man of the dust of the ground, and breathed into his nostrils the breath of life; and man became a living being.

Job 27:3 As long as my breath is in me, and the breath of God in my nostrils,

Job 33:4 The Spirit of God has made me, and the breath of the Almighty gives me life.

Psalm 104:29,30 You hide Your face, they are troubled; You take away their breath, they die and return to their dust. You send forth Your Spirit, they are created; and You renew the face of the earth.

Isaiah 42:5 Thus says God the LORD, who created the heavens and stretched them out, who spread forth the earth and that which comes from it, who gives breath to the people on it, and spirit to those who walk on it:

Creation Of Man.

Man was created in the image and likeness of God, embodies a tripartite nature of spirit, soul, and body, much like that of The Father, The Son, The Holy Spirit. Man was created for the purpose of being the image bearer of God, displaying the exact likeness of God and originally righteousness. Man was destined for immortality, and as male and female, they share equality yet differ in purpose, form, and function, destined to unite as one. Man was entrusted with dominion over the earth, displaying creativity, emotions, and supernatural wisdom. However, the fall of man into sin shattered this plan incurring judgment. From that point forward all people are now born into a world of sin and become partakers of sin and enemies of God. Only through the completed wok of Jesus Christ is redemption freely available, which restores the promises of the reason for man being created.

Isaiah 43:7, Everyone who is called by my name, whom I created for My glory, whom I formed and made.

Genesis 1:26,27 "Then God said, "Let us make man in our image, in our likeness... So God created man in his own image, in the image of God he created him; male and female he created them.

The Fall Of Man.

Genesis 3:6 So when the woman saw that the tree was good for food, that it was pleasant to the eyes, and a tree desirable to make one wise, she took of its fruit and ate. She also gave to her husband with her, and he ate. The fall of man is recorded almost immediately after the creation accounts, though how much time passed between when God made mankind and when Adam and Eve sinned is unknown. It could have been a few hours or many years.

Genesis 2, tells about how God created man in His own image. His own image means that God and man share some attributes, but not all.

God placed Adam in the Garden of Eden, and was sent down to Earth from Heaven. In Heaven the Garden of Eden was called the Garden of God.

God, told Adam that he could eat of any tree except one: the tree of knowledge of good and evil or else Adam would die. This indicates that God gave man free will to choose to trust God or rebel against God.

God then created a female as a helpmate - a wife - of Adam, giving us the divine institute of marriage. Adam called her woman after the fall and then called the woman Eve.

The serpent who is Satan approached Eve and twisted God's word in order to convince her to eat the forbidden fruit. In Genesis 3:1 Satan said to Eve, 'Did God actually say...'
In Satan saying this to Eve, he was challenging her on the identity she had, being created in the image of God.
When Eve chose to entertain the deception of Satan, he then played mind games with her by outright denying God's word and claiming God was withholding things from her and Adam. Satan claimed, "You will not surely die," and that if she ate, "you will be like God" Genesis 3:4,5 Then the serpent said to the woman, You will not surely die. For God knows that in the day you eat of it your eyes will be opened, and you will be like God, knowing good and evil.
Eve, now probably questioning God's motives, was now enticed,

After they sinned, they immediately realized what they did, so they tried in vain to fix it or cover it up.
Genesis 3:7 Then the eyes of both of them were opened, and they knew that they were naked, and they sewed fig leaves together and made themselves coverings.

However, God already knew what they did. Also, while he would have been well within his rights to immediately strike them dead, he chose instead to show grace by giving them a chance to repent.

God killed an animal and used the skin to create a covering for Adam and Eve's nakedness.
Genesis 3:21 Also for Adam and his wife the LORD God made tunics of skin and clothed them.

After the fall of man, God drove Adam and Eve out of the garden of Eden and placed the cherubim as guard of the garden to ensure that they were never able to return.
Genesis 3:23,24 therefore the LORD God sent him out of the garden of Eden to till the ground from which he was taken. So He drove out the man; and He placed cherubim at the east of the garden of Eden, and a flaming sword which turned every way, to guard the way to the tree of life.

The Fourfold Judgment Incurred Through The Fall Of Man:
1. Upon the serpent. The curse of degradation.
    Micah 7:17, They will lick dust like a snake, like creatures that crawl on the ground. They will come trembling out of their dens; they will turn in fear to the LORD our God and will be afraid of you.
2. Upon the woman. The judgment of pain in birth and subjection to man.

John 16:21, A woman giving birth to a child has pain because her time has come...

3. Upon the man. The judgment of sorrow and toil.

   Ecclesiastes 2:22,23, "What does a man get for all the toil and anxious striving with which he labors under the sun?"

4. Upon the ground. Isa 55:13, "Instead of the thorn bush will grow the pine tree, and instead of briers the myrtle will grow."

The Threefold Separation Incurred Through The Fall Of Man:

1. From the tree of life. Revelation 2:7 He who has an ear, let him hear what the Spirit says to the churches. To him who overcomes I will give to eat from the tree of life, which is in the midst of the Paradise of God.

2. From the Garden of Eden. Genesis 3:24, After He drove the man out, He placed on the east side of the Garden of Eden cherubim and a flaming sword flashing back and forth to guard the way to the tree of life.

3. From the personal and visible presence of God. Isaiah 59:2 Your sins have separated from your God and made His face hide from you.

The Threefold Death Incurred Through The Fall Of Man:

1. Physical death. The separation from soul/spirit from body.

I Corinthians 15:21 For since death came through a man, the resurrection of the dead comes also through a man."

2. Spiritual death. The separation of soul/spirit from God.

    Romans 8:13, For if you live according to the sinful nature, you will die; but if by the Spirit you put to death the misdeeds of the body, you will live.

3. Eternal death. 2 Thessalonians 1:9, They will be punished with everlasting destruction and shut out from the presence of the Lord and from the majesty of his power.

DOCTRINE OF FAITH

It is impossible to not have faith.

Even choosing to be an agnostic, one needs faith to believe in agnosticism. Charles H Spurgeon said; One walking with me, observed, with some emphasis, "I do not believe as you do. I am an agnostic." "Oh," I said to him, "that is a Greek word, is it not? The Latin word, I think, is 'ignoramus' ". He did not like that at all. Yet I only translated his language from Greek to Latin. These are queer waters to get into, when all your philosophy brings you is the confession that you know nothing, and the stupidity which enables you to glory in your ignorance.

Faith pleases God; Hebrews 11;6 'without faith it is impossible to please God'

1. The faith of God is greater than the faith of man.
2. God has more faith in you than you have faith in God.

BIBLE DOCTRINE

Definition Of Faith

Hebrews 11:1 Faith is the substance of things hoped for, the evidence of things not seen.

1. Faith is the connecting power into the spiritual realm.
2. Faith is the ingredient to begin a relationship with God.
3. Faith is the evidence of those things that are not yet visible.
4. Faith is the reality.
5. God is Alpha and Omega – when God speaks in the future tense – the act has already happened. (I will bless you, by faith has already happened)

Hebrew: the verb is AMAN (aw-man) - to believe, to support, to use someone as a prop, a crutch; to use someone else to be supported, The root meaning is a foundation on which you build something.

Greek; the verb is PISTUEO - the root word from which we get 'faith, the noun is PISTIS, and 'believe',

BIBLE DOCTRINE

The Four Kinds Of Faith.

1. Human faith - head faith. Human faith that is inherent within every human being, and there is a supernatural faith of God that only comes to those who receive the good news. Human faith can only believe what it can see, taste, hear, smell, or feel; it's limited to the five senses. Using natural human faith, we can sit in a chair we've never sat in and believe it will hold us up. We fly in airplanes when we don't fully understand how they work, and we don't know the pilot, but we trust that everything will be okay. That takes human faith, which God gave to every person. You can't believe in invisible things with human faith.

2. Faith for salvation – Heart faith. – Ephesians 2:8, Paul says, "For by grace are ye saved through faith; and Romans 12:3 says, "God has given to every man equal measure of faith"

3. Gift of faith – faith to trust God for above and beyond.

4. God's faith – Faith of God in Himself to do what He said He will do. Have the Faith of God is 5 times in scripture.

    1. Romans 10;17 So then faith comes by hearing, and hearing by the word of God.
    2. Galatians 2;9. 'I live in faith, the faith which is in the Son of God'
    3. Philippians 3; 20 - 'but that which is through faith in Christ.
    4. Mark 11;22 'Have the faith of God'
    5. Hebrews 6;19. hope we have as an anchor of the soul,

Importance Of Faith

It is impossible to be saved without faith.

Hebrews 11: 6 But without faith it is impossible to please Him, for he who comes to God must believe that He is, and that He is a rewarder of those who diligently seek Him.

Everything life is attained through faith. It is faith carries you in the natural realm and it is faith which is the bridge between the now and the latter.

Five principals of faith to learn from Abrahams faith.

1. Abraham heard the Word.

    Romans 4:13 For the promise that he would be the heir of the world was not to Abraham or to his seed through the law, but through the righteousness of faith.

2. Abraham turned and repented.

    Romans 4:18 who, contrary to hope, in hope believed,

3. Abraham embraced the hope.

    Romans 4:19 And not being weak in faith, …

4. Abraham did not waver in faith.

    Romans 4:20 He did not waver at the promise of God through unbelief, but was strengthened in faith,

5. Abraham rejoiced in the completed work.

    Romans 4:20 giving glory to God,

Work Of Faith

The work of faith is revealed in Romans 4:3 'Abraham believed God, and it was accounted to him for righteousness', and it needs to be obtained, held onto, believed in, and be the foundation of abiding in Him.

1. Obtain precious faith through righteousness of God.
   2 Peter 1:1 To those who have obtained like precious faith with us by the righteousness of our God and Savior Jesus Christ...
2. God is the author and finisher of our faith. Hebrews 12:2 'Looking unto Jesus, the author and finisher of our faith,..."
3. Faith is the substance through which we receive from God. Hebrews11;1 Now faith is the substance of things hoped for, the evidence of things not seen.
4. Saved through Faith, not of yourselves. Ephesians 2: 8 For by grace you have been saved through faith, and that not of yourselves; it is the gift of God,

BIBLE DOCTRINE

Act In Faith

The act of faith is complete reliance in the faith of God.

Philippians 1:6 I am sure of this, that He who started a good work in you will carry it on to completion until the day of Christ Jesus.

Proverbs 3;5 Trust in the Lord with all your heart and lean not to your own understanding

1. Lays hold of God's resources, becomes obedient to what He has prescribed and putting aside all self-interest and self-reliance, trusts Him completely.
2. Total complete unqualified surrender of being in dependence upon Him.
3. Total complete trusting reliance upon Him for all things.
4. Faith in action comes from a deep inner conviction. -

BIBLE DOCTRINE

Four Foundations For Biblical Faith.

1. Knowing in who you believe. 1 TIMOTHY 1:12 I know whom I have believed and am persuaded that He is able to keep what I have committed to Him until that Day.
2. Knowing that God can never lie. Numbers 23:19 God is not a man, that He should lie,...
3. Guarantee of God' promise. Romans 4:21 ... being fully convinced that what He had promised He was also able to perform.
4. Confidence in The Promise. Joshua 1;9 Be strong and of good courage; do not be afraid, nor be dismayed, for the LORD your God is with you wherever you go.

BIBLE DOCTRINE

Three Hindrances To Faith

1. Absence of the Word and the sower and 4 types of soil. Matthew 13:3-9 Behold, a sower went out to sow. And as he sowed, some seed fell by the wayside; and the birds came and devoured them. Some fell on stony places, where they did not have much earth; and they immediately sprang up because they had no depth of earth. But when the sun was up they were scorched, and because they had no root they withered away. And some fell among thorns, and the thorns sprang up and choked them. But others fell on good ground and yielded a crop: some a hundredfold, some sixty, some thirty. He who has ears to hear, let him hear!.
    1. Good soil – receiving heart.
    2. Hard soil – hard heart.
    3. Stony soil - no depth of spiritual life.
    4. Thorny soil - cares of this life.
2. Wrong Motivation - Matthew 6;33 Seek first the kingdom of God and His righteousness,

    James 4: 3-4 You ask and you do not receive because..
3. Wrong Source of Knowledge - Confusing human faith and the 5 senses: (seeing, hearing, tasting, smelling and touching) with salvation faith, gift of faith and God faith.

FOUNDATIONS OF FAITH

BIBLE DOCTRINE

DOCTRINE OF SALVATION

Salvation in Greek is Soteria and this word is derived from the word soter which means savior.

The doctrine of Salvation is also called Soteriology, and the understanding of salvation and soteriology is:

Soteriology is the greatest theme in all scripture.
Soteriology embraces all of eternity past, present, and future.
Soteriology relates to all of mankind, without exception.
Soteriology has ramifications in the sphere of the angels.
Soteriology is the main theme of both the Old and New Testaments.
Soteriology is personal, national, and cosmic.
Soteriology centers on the Lord Jesus Christ.
Soteriology encompasses the total work of God seeking to rescue man from sin and bestow upon man His Grace encompassing eternal life.

Ephesians 1:3-8 Blessed is he who reads and those who hear the words of this prophecy, and keep those things which are written in it; for the time is near. Grace to you and peace from Him who is and who was and who is to come, and from the seven Spirits who are before His throne, and from

Jesus Christ, the faithful witness, the firstborn from the dead, and the ruler over the kings of the earth. To Him who loved us and washed us from our sins in His own blood, and has made us kings and priests to His God and Father, to Him be glory and dominion forever and ever. Amen. Behold, He is coming with clouds, and every eye will see Him, even they who pierced Him. And all the tribes of the earth will mourn because of Him. Even so, Amen. "I am the Alpha and the Omega, the Beginning and the End," says the Lord, "who is and who was and who is to come, the Almighty."

Vocabulary And Definition Of Salvation.

1. Conversion.

    Psalms 19:7 the law of the Lord is perfect, converting the soul.

    Definition;

    Hebrew word shuv, means to turn back or return.

    Greek words epistrepho and metanoeo, both mean to turn away from self and sin and turn to God.

    Metanoia can also be translated as repentance.

2. Repentance. Greek: Metanoia.

    Definition; "to turn from evil, and to turn to the good."

    Ezekiel 14:6 'This is what the Sovereign LORD says: Repent! Turn from your idols and renounce all your detestable practices!

    The most common term in the Old Testament for repentance appears over 1,050 times, and over 33 times in the New Testament.

a. Repentance is not turning over a new leaf.

   b. Repentance is not remorse.

   c. Repentance is not penitence.

   d. Repentance is confessing sin.

   e. Repentance is asking for forgiveness from sin.

   f. Repentance is receiving the forgiveness of sin.

   g. Repentance is turning from the sin and not going back to it.

3. Substitution. Christ is our substitution for the judgement of our sin.

   1 Peter 3:18 For Christ has once suffered for our sins, just for the unjust, that He might bring us to God.

4. Reconciliation. Literally means to change completely. Greek; Allasso. Reconciliation, has to do with the relationships between God and man or man and man.

   2 Corinthians 5:18 God has reconciled the world, not counting people's sins against them. Reconciliation is also related to justification.

5. Justification. The remission of sin and absolution from guilt and punishment; or an act of free grace by which God pardons the sinner and accepts him as righteous, on account of the atonement of Christ. Romans 5. We have been justified through faith (v. 1) by his blood (v. 9).

6. Propitiation. The act of appeasing the wrath of God through the atoning sacrifice of Jesus Christ offered to God for the assuage of His wrath and render Him propitious to sinners. Christ is the propitiation for the sins of men.

7. Remission. The act of exempting, absolving and remitting from the consequences of sin and offenses against God. Remission is restricted to the penalty, while forgiveness refers more particularly to the person, although it may be used also of the sin itself.

8. Forgiveness. God's restoration of relationship and the removal of guilt. The three most common verbs for forgiveness.
    a. Salah (swa-lakh): to forgive and to pardon.
    b. Kapar (kaw-far): to make atonement and reconciliation.
    c. Nasa (naw-saw): to lift, to bear up, to carry and to take off.

9. Redemption. The action of saving or being saved from sin, deception, error, or evil, and the action of regaining or gaining possession of something in exchange for payment, or clearing a debt.

10. Regeneration. The impartation of divine life which is manifested in that radical change in the moral character of man, from the love and life of sin to the love of God and the life of righteousness.

11. Imputation. The act of assigning a condition, standing, or value. When it relates to persons, the new condition is credited to them, and accounted as being fully theirs. The sin of Adam was imputed to us long ago. The righteousness of Jesus Christ is imputed (credited) to all those redeemed by him on the Cross of Calvary. There our sin was imputed to our Savior where the demands of its guilt were satisfied before God forever.

12. Adoption. The act of leaving one's natural family and entering into the privileges and responsibilities of another family.

13. Supplication. The act of humble and earnest prayer, petitioning, pleading and intreating with God in prayer as in worship.
14. Preservation. The act of keeping and saving from injury or destruction and defending from evil.
15. Conviction. The work of the Holy Spirit, where a person is able to see himself as God sees him: guilty, sinful, defiled, and unable to save himself.
16. Sanctification. The means to set apart for special use or purpose, to make holy and make sacred as a vessel, full of the Holy Spirit of God. Sanctification is the highest goal of the work of God.
17. Preservation. To keep or save from injury or destruction; to defend from evil.
18. Glorification. The final stage of soteriology and eschatology that can attained and lived to the full while on earth before leaving earth.

Reasons For Salvation:
1. Salvation reveals His love.
2. Salvation shows the non-meritorious favor of God.
3. Salvation is because men are lost;
    a) They are lost because of their rejection to biblical revelation.
    b) They are lost because of disobeying their conscience.
    c) They are lost because of their relationship to the world.
    d) They are lost because of their relationship to Satan.

BIBLE DOCTRINE

e) They are lost because of their relationship too son.

f) They are lost because of their relationship to God.

Three Tenses Of Salvation:

1. Past tense is justification from the penalty of sin.

   Ephesians 2:8 For by grace you have been saved through faith, and that not of yourselves; it is the gift of God,

2. Present tense is sanctification over sin.

   1 Corinthians 1:18 For the message of the cross is foolishness to those who are perishing, but to us who are being saved it is the power of God.

3. Future tense glorification in deliverance from sin.

   1 Peter 1:5 who are kept by the power of God through faith for salvation ready to be revealed in the last time.

Arminiasm And Calvinism

Salvation according to Arminianism: Salvation is accomplished through the combined efforts of God (who takes the initiative) and man (who must respond) - man's response being the determining factor. God has provided salvation for everyone, but His provision becomes effective only for those who, of their own free will, "choose" to cooperate with Him and accept His offer of grace. At the crucial point, man's will plays a decisive role; thus man, not God, determines who will be recipients of the gift of salvation.

Salvation according to Calvinism: Salvation is accomplished by the almighty power of God. The Father, God The Son and God The Holy Spirit. The Father chose a people; The Son died for them and The Holy Spirit makes Christ the Son's death effective by bringing the elect to faith and repentance, thereby causing them to willingly obey the gospel. The entire process (election, redemption, regeneration) is the work of God and is by grace alone. Thus God, not man, determines who will be the recipients of the gift of salvation.

Steps For Salvation:

1. Hear the Gospel of Christ. Romans 10:17
2. Confess of your sins. 1 John 1:9
3. Believe that Jesus Christ is the Son of God. John 8:24
4. Be baptized in water. Mark 16:16
5. Be filled with the Holy Spirit. Ephesians 5:18

Result Of Salvation

1. Reconciliation: We were enemies of God but we were reconciled to God through the death of His Son, having been reconciled, we shall be saved by His death.

2. Regeneration: The Spirit of God indwells a repentant sinner and imparts eternal life to his or her spiritually dead soul.
3. Justification: is the divine act of declaring sinners to be righteous on account of their faith in Jesus Christ.
4. Sanctification: is the process in which God develops the new life of a believer and gradually brings it to perfection.
5. Glorification: is the ultimate salvation of the whole person. (to make <u>glorious</u> by bestowing honor, praise, or admiration)
6. Adoption: for as many as are led by the Spirit of God, these are Sons of God. The Spirit Himself bears witness with our spirit that we are children of God, and if children of God, then heirs—heirs of God and joint heirs with Christ, if indeed we suffer with Him, that we may also be glorified together.

Christians Can Lose Their Salvation

We must understand that salvation is eternal, though salvation can be lost:

1. The will of the Father is that every believer is to be eternally secure in their salvation.
John 10:28,29 And I give them eternal life, and they shall never perish; neither shall anyone snatch them out of My hand. My Father, who has given them to Me, is greater than all; and no one is able to snatch them out of My Father's hand.

2. God is married to the backslider.

    Jeremiah 3:14 Return, O backsliding children," says the LORD; "for I am married to you. I will take you, one from a city and two from a family, and I will bring you to Zion.

The prophetic story of Icahbod in 1 Samuel, chapters 2 and 4 reveals how a Christian can lose their salvation.

1. Israel had lost the fear of God.
2. Hophni and Phinehas died in battle when the Philistines captured the Ark of the Covenant.
3. Eli fell backward off his chair and broke his neck and died.
4. Phinehas's pregnant wife went into labor and bore a son.
5. She named the child Ichabod, then died.
6. The presence of God never departed from the Ark of Covenant even while the ark of the covenant was in captivity.
7. Israel's lack of fear for God was the down fall for Israel and showed their rejection of their Messiah.

    Matthew 23:37,38 Jesus last message refers to the glory of God leaving Israel. 'O Jerusalem, Jerusalem, you who kill the prophets and stone those sent to you, how often I have longed to gather your children together, as a hen gathers her chicks under her wings, but you were not willing. Look, your house is left to you desolate'.

    a. Jesus did not say 'My house was left desolate, Jesus said 'your house is desolate'.

b. What Jesus was saying is 'You broke the relationship, you separated yourself from God.'

Moving From Salvation To Perfection
1. Salvation gives you the guarantee of going to Heaven.
2. Working out your salvation with fear trembling, gives you the surety of going to Heaven as a perfect man, to the measure of the stature of the fullness of Christ.

Philippians 2:12 Work out your salvation with fear and trembling.

Ephesians 4:13 Till we all come to the unity of the faith and of the knowledge of the Son of God, to a perfect man, to the measure of the stature of the fullness of Christ;

Commitments to personal growth toward perfection
1. Seek The Face of God. Desire to know God.
2. Seek The Glory of God. Desire to experience the Power and anointing of God.
3. Pray privately daily and join in corporate prayer.
4. Read the Bible daily and memorize scripture.
5. Fast often and position yourself to receive more from God.
6. Do justly as you impact the seven spheres of society.
7. Give extravagantly and experience financial power encounters.

8. Live holy in loving God that overflows to loving people.
9. Lead diligently in outreaches, prayer meetings, and Bible studies.
10. Witness boldly in word and action.
11. Ask God to remove and expose to you the hinderances in your life that separate you from seeking The Face of God and following through on the other commitments to God.

DOCTRINE OF ANGELS

An angel by definition is a messenger. The Bible has over three hundred references to angels, and defines two groups of angelic messengers. Heavenly angels carry out the commands of God, while fallen angels carry out acts of deceit and wickedness.

Angels are mentioned in 34 books of the Bible for a total of 273 times. 108 times in the OT and 165 times in the NT.

The word angel (Hebrew "Malak", Greek "Angeles") signifies a messenger – one sent to deliver a message – an ambassador sent to bring tidings.

The Origin Of Angels:

1. Angels like everything else in the universe were created by God through Jesus Christ in the power of the Holy Spirit.

   Nehemiah 9:6 You alone are the LORD; You have made heaven,

   The heaven of heavens, with all their hosts. John 1:3 All things were made through Him, and without Him nothing was made that was made.

2. All angels are created beings, they are not evolved beings and neither are they born through procreation.

   Psalms 148:2 Praise Him, all His angels; Praise Him, all His hosts!

3. Each angel is a direct creation individual creation from God. This is why angels are referred to as Sons of God.

4. Angels were created at creation and they are a fixed number in their quantity forever, and they do not reproduce

5. Angels can never die and they numbers will never increase or decrease.

6. Angels are considered to be a company of beings and not a race.

The Nature Of Angels:

1. Angels are created "spirit beings" – created by God.

   Colossians 1:16 For by Him all things were created that are in heaven and that are on earth, visible and invisible, whether thrones or dominions or principalities or powers. All things were created through Him and for Him.

2. Angels are invisible beings.

3. Angels constantly surround us.

4. Angels are in-numerable.

5. Angels possess separate and individual personalities and more than likely, there are not two the same.

6. Angels are greater than man in power and might.

7. Just one angel killed 185,000 men of the Assyrian army in a single night.

8. Angels are smarter than men.

9. They are always spoken of in the masculine gender and are never given in marriage.

10. Angels neither marry nor die.

11. Angels are not omniscient. Although they have great knowledge yet there are many things they do not know.

12. Angels must not be worshipped.

13. Angels are classed in different ranks or orders.

14. Angels are subject to The Lord Jesus Christ and are created to worship Him.

15. Angels are spoken of as HOLY and God will not tolerate uncleanness (sin) amongst their ranks.

16. Angels will be judged by believers.

17. Angels eat!

18. Angels can take on human form.

19. Angels do not need rest.

20. Angels protect God's people.

21. Angels speak their own language.

22. Angels ascend and descend from heaven.

23. Angels learn the wisdom of God by observing God's people.

Classification And Rank Of Angels.

The Bible does not reveal an angelic hierarchy. God is the commander of His heavenly host (Isaiah 45:12). However, there are a few scriptures that infer delegated authority to some angels. Paul mentions "elect angels" (I Timothy 5:21) and says that "one star differs from another star in glory" (I Corinthians 15:41), implying that each star (and each angel) is unique in glory and in position. Though it is noted that angels do differing functions and responsibilities.

1. ArchAngels:

The word archangel is mentioned twice in Scripture. The Greek word is archaggelos which is a combination of archo (meaning "first" in political rank or power) and aggelos (meaning "messenger"). An archangel by definition is the first or highest angel and leader of the angels.

   a. Michael - His name means: Who is like God.

   b. Gabriel - His name means: The mighty one of God who is the chief prince.

   c. Besides Michael and Gabriel, apocryphal books and historical documents mention names of other angels. The Bible makes reference to seven angels in Revelation (1:20, 3:1, 4:5, 8:2, and 10:7) who have been placed over the seven churches and also carry out the seven judgments on the earth. These may be the seven archangels named in extra-biblical writings. The Book of Enoch tells of seven powerful angels (20:1-8). Uriel, who is set over the world and over Tartarus; Raphael, who is set over the spirits of men; Raguel, who takes vengeance on the world of the luminaries; Michael, who is set over the best part of mankind, over chaos, and over Israel; Saraqael, who is set over the evil spirits; Gabriel, who is set over Paradise, the serpents (seraphim), and the cherubim; and Remiel, whom God set over those who rise.

2. Cherubim: These are guardian angels to the entrance of paradise and the Holy of Holies. It is interesting to see the analogy of the winged bulls and lions of Babylon and Asyria, the colosal figures with human faces that guard the entrance of the temples and palaces. The location of these statues is the original place of the garden of Eden. It Is not unreasonable to suggest that these statues are false idols and copies of the real cherubims. Exodus 25:18-20 – Prior to the fall of Satan, Lucifer was the chief cherub angel. Isaiah 14:12, Ezek. 28:14

3. Serahim: (means the burning one) These creatures are mentioned only once in the bible. Isaiah 6:3 They have an intense passion of devotion to God. They have 6 wings and Isaiah was ministered to by one of the cherubim who touched his tongue with a coal from the Alta of God.

4. Living Creatures: Revelation 4:6-9, 5:8, 6:1 These creatures are similar to that of the Seraphim and the Cherubim, though there number seems limited to 4.

5. Ruling Angels: Ephesians1:21, 3:10, There are six distinct categories among the Ruling Angels and it seems that the analogy is that to military ranking, generals to privates.

    a. Ruling Angels over Principalities.

    b. Ruling Angels over Powers.

    c. Ruling Angels over Thrones.

d. Ruling Angels over Authorities.

   e. Ruling Angels over Dominions.

   f. Ruling Angels over Might.

6. Guardian Angels: Hebrews 1:14, Mt. 18:10   The bible does not state if each believer has their own personal guardian angel or not if there are guardian angels for communities.

7. Angels associated with horses and chariots: Psalms 68:17, Zecheriah 1:8-11   It is most probable these angels are war, work, and stately angels that are created to bring Glory to God along-side the creatures of the animal kingdom.

Angelic Visitations

1. Abraham receives a visit. Genesis 18:1-8 Then the LORD appeared to Abraham at the oaks of Mamre while he was sitting in the entrance of his tent during the heat of the day. He looked up, and he saw three men standing near him. When he saw them, he ran from the entrance of the tent to meet them and bowed to the ground. Then he said, "My lord, if I have found favor in your sight, please do not go on past your servant. Let a little water be brought, that you may wash your feet and rest yourselves under the tree. I will bring a bit of bread so that you may strengthen yourselves. This

is why you have passed your servant's way. Later, you can continue on." "Yes," they replied, "do as you have said." So Abraham hurried into the tent and said to Sarah, "Quick! Knead three measures of fine flour and make bread." Meanwhile, Abraham ran to the herd and got a tender, choice calf. He gave it to a young man, who hurried to prepare it. Then Abraham took curds and milk, and the calf that he had prepared, and set them before the men. He served them as they ate under the tree.

2. Jacob saw angels. Genesis 32:1-2 Jacob went on his way, and God's angels met him. When he saw them, Jacob said, "This is God's camp." So he called that place Mahanaim.

3. Elijah was touched by an angel and is provided supernaturally with a meal. 1 Kings 19:4-8 but he went on a day's journey into the wilderness. He sat down under a broom tree and prayed that he might die. He said, "I have had enough! LORD, take my life, for I'm no better than my fathers." Then he lay down and slept under the broom tree. Suddenly, an angel touched him. The angel told him, "Get up and eat." Then he looked, and there at his head was a loaf of bread baked over hot stones, and a jug of water. So he ate and drank and lay down again. Then the angel of the LORD returned for a second time and touched him. He said, "Get up and eat, or the journey will be too much for you."

4. Elisha and Gehazi see the heavenly hosts. 2 Kings 6:17 Then Elisha prayed, " LORD, please open his eyes and let him see." So the LORD

opened the servant's eyes. He looked and saw that the mountain was covered with horses and chariots of fire all around Elisha.

5. Zechariah saw an angel. Luke 1:11 An angel of the Lord appeared to him, standing to the right of the altar of incense. When Zechariah saw him, he was startled and overcome with fear.

6. The shepherds saw many angels. Luke 2:9-14 Suddenly there was a multitude of the heavenly host with the angel, praising God and saying:

7. Jesus was ministered to by angels. Matthew 4:11 "....Angels came and ministered unto Him".

8. Jesus was served by angels. Mark 1:13 He was in the wilderness 40 days, being tempted by Satan. He was with the wild animals, and the angels began to serve Him.

9. An angel opened prison doors for the apostles . Acts 5:18,19 So they arrested the apostles and put them in the city jail. But an angel of the Lord opened the doors of the jail during the night, brought them out, and said,

10. The Angel speaks to Philip: Acts 8:26. Go hear – join thyself to this chariot.

11. Cornelius receives a visitation. Acts 10:3 About three in the afternoon he distinctly saw in a vision an angel of God who came in and said to him, "Cornelius!"

12. Peter in prison is visitation. Acts 12:7 Suddenly an angel of the Lord appeared, and a light shone in the cell. Striking Peter on the side, he

woke him up and said, "Quick, get up!" Then the chains fell off his wrists.

13. Herod was struck by an angel. Acts 12:23 At once an angel of the Lord struck him because he did not give the glory to God, and he became infected with worms and died.

14. Angel appears to Paul and speaks to Him. Acts 27:23 For this night an angel of the God I belong to and serve stood by me,

15. Jesus could ask His Father to send angels. Matthew 26:53 Or do you think that I cannot call on My Father, and He will provide Me at once with more than 12 legions of angels? (Legion – 3,000 to up ward of 5,000).

At death angels take God's people to their new abode. Luke 16:22 One day the poor man died and was carried away by the angels to Abraham's side.

DOCTRINE OF SATAN

There is barely a culture, tribe, community, nation or society to be found in the world who do not have some form of concept or fear of an invisible evil power that seeks out to destroy them and have them find their eternity separated from God.

Satan who is Lucifer is the chief of devils, is mentioned in seven books of the Old Testament, in nineteen books of the New Testament, and also mentioned by Jesus fifteen times.

The Origin Of Satan:

Lucifer was created by God to be the angel who would be the image bearer of God, full of wisdom, bejeweled with every precious stone, the finest of gold, having worship created with within him, all treasures and wealth woven into his clothing.

He was created as the anointed guardian cherub that covers the holy holies.

He was flawless in every way, until he made a decision to rise above God.

It was at this point that Satan corrupted his own wisdom and defiled his beauty for the sake of splendor. Then God cast Satan down to be despised by all.

Ezekiel 28:12-19 This is what the Lord GOD says: You were the seal of perfection, full of wisdom and perfect in beauty. You were in Eden, the garden of God. Every kind of precious stone covered you: carnelian, topaz, and diamond, beryl, onyx, and jasper, sapphire, turquoise and emerald. Your mountings and settings were crafted in gold; they were prepared on the day you were created. You were an anointed guardian cherub, for I had appointed you. You were on the holy mountain of God; you walked among the fiery stones. From the day you were created you were blameless in your ways until wickedness was found in you. Through the abundance of your trade, you were filled with violence, and you sinned. So I expelled you in disgrace from the mountain of God, and banished you, guardian cherub, from among the fiery stones. Your heart became proud because of your beauty; For the sake of your splendor, you corrupted your wisdom. So I threw you down to the earth; I made you a spectacle before kings. You profaned your sanctuaries by the magnitude of your iniquities in your dishonest trade. So I made fire come from within you, and it consumed you. I reduced you to ashes on the ground in the sight of everyone watching you. All those who know you among the nations are appalled at you. You have become an object of horror and will never exist again."

When Lucifer was cast out from Eden the Garden of God, he lost his role as guardian cherub and today he is the counterfeit lion, calf, eagle, and man as spoken of Revelation 4:7 The first living creature was like a lion; the second living creature was like a calf; the third living creature had a face like a man; and the fourth living creature was like a flying eagle.

Jesus Christ is the true representation in Revelation 4:7 and is pictured in the four gospels as:

a. Matthew presents Christ as the lion-like King.

b. Mark presents Christ as the calf-like servant.

c. Luke presents Christ as the perfect man.

d. John presents Christ as the eagle-like God.

The Word of God says in Romans 16:20 'The God of peace will soon crush Satan under your feet' and in Ephesians 6;12 "we wrestle not against flesh and blood, but against principalities, against powers, against the rulers of the darkness of this world, against spiritual wickedness in high places."

The word principalities in the above scripture are taken from the Greek word archai, which is used symbolically to depict individuals who hold the highest position of rank and authority.

To clearly understand who our enemy is, we need to look deeper into Ephesians 6:12 and the workings of his kingdom and authority.
The word 'powers; is taken from the Greek word exousia, and it denotes delegated authority. This is the second level of demon spirits who have received delegated authority from Satan to carry out all manner of

evil in whatever way they desire to do it. These evil forces are second in command in Satan's dark kingdom.

The phrase 'rulers of the darkness of this world' is taken from the Greek word komokrateros and is a compound of the words kosmos and kratos.

The word kosmos denotes order or arrangement, whereas the word kratos has to do with raw power. Thus, the compounded word kosmokrateros depicts raw power that has been harnessed and put into some kind of order.

The spiritual wickedness in high places.

The word "wickedness" is taken from the word poneros, and it is used to depict something that is bad, vile, malevolent, vicious, impious, and malignant. This tells us the ultimate aim of Satan's dark domain: These evil spirits are sent forth to afflict humanity in bad, vile, malevolent, and vicious ways!

The Fall Of Satan:

It is most important to know that satan is a fallen angel, who is cast out of heaven.

Isaiah 14: 13,14 You said to yourself: "I will ascend to the heavens;

I will set up my throne above the stars of God. I will sit on the mount of the gods' assembly, in the remotest parts of the North. I will ascend above the highest clouds; I will make myself like the Most High."

Satan had only one thing he desired from God and that was to take all the power from God for himself. Satan did not desire any of the attributes of God, such as the many-breasted one, or the provider, or the all-knowing, or the banner, or refuge or healer, no satan wanted to be like El-Elyon the Most High. Satan wanted to be the most powerful strongest strong one.

Satan said his fatal 5 "I will's" of arrogance and pride that led to his downfall.

1) I will ascend into the heaven.
2) I will exalt my throne above the stars of God.
3) I will sit on the mount of the congregation.
4) I will ascend above the heights of the clouds.
5) I will be like the most High.

When Satan rose his fist against God, The Lord rose up a standard against Satan cast him down. Satan's Geographical Locations

Satan is geographical location is divided into the past the present and the future.

Satan's geographical location in the past;

1. On the Heavens and on the Mountain of God. Ezekiel 28:14 You were on the holy mountain of God;
2. you walked among the fiery stones
3. On earth. Isaiah 14;12 Shining morning star, how you have fallen from the heavens! You destroyer of nations, you have been cut down to the ground.

Satan's geographical location in the present;

4. In the Heavenlies as the chief enemy of God and man. Job 1:7 The LORD asked Satan, "Where have you come from?" "From roaming through the earth," Satan answered Him, "and walking around on it."
5. On earth. Luke 10;18 I watched Satan fall from heaven like a lightning flash.

Satan's geographical location in the future;

6. On Earth for the last time, after the 1000 yrs of peace. Revelation 20:7-9 When the 1,000 years are completed, Satan will be released from his prison and will go out to deceive the nations at the four corners of the earth, Gog and Magog, to gather them for battle. Their number is like the sand of the sea. They came up over the surface of the earth and surrounded the encampment of the saints, the beloved city. Then fire came down from heaven and consumed them.
7. The lake of fire. Revelation 20:10 The Devil who deceived them was thrown into the lake of fire and sulfur where the beast and the false

prophet are, and they will be tormented day and night forever and ever.

BIBLE DOCTRINE

The kingdom of Satan is divided into 7 sub-kingdoms

Quote from Derek Prince,

"Our wrestling match is not against persons with bodies. But against rulerships with various areas and descending orders of authority, against the world dominators of this present darkness, against spiritual hosts of wickedness in the heavenlies." What I want to point out to you is that Satan's kingdom is no jumble; it is a highly-organized kingdom, for which he gets no credit because he was, one of the chief angels in charge of a large section of the angels. And as such he had a divinely given organizational system. And when he rebelled against God and led his angels in rebellion he simply took the system with him but turned it against God. So don't imagine that Satan does not have a highly organized kingdom. For which, as I said, he gets no credit. The credit goes to God. But let us take into account the fact that he is no simpleton. He is a very astute, powerful and evil being.'

The seven sub-kingdoms of satan:

1. The occult kingdom on earth.

2. The water kingdom is ruled by water spirits of all waters. Revelation 12:12 ... Woe to the earth and the sea, for the Devil has come down to you.

3. The Occult Kingdom is ruled by angels of death. 2 Chronicles 33:6 He passed his sons through the fire in the Valley of Hinnom. He practiced witchcraft, divination, and sorcery, and consulted mediums and spirits. He did a great deal of evil in the LORD'S sight, provoking Him.

4. The Astral kingdom gives direct access to satan. Ephesians 2:2 in which you previously walked according to the ways of this world, according to the ruler who exercises authority over the lower heavens, the spirit now working in the disobedient.

5. The terrestrial kingdom of the air is ruled by demi-gods, and is known as the middle heavens. Ephesians 2:2...according to the ruler who exercises authority over the lower heavens, the spirit now working in the disobedient.

6. The azura kingdom of the air operates in mystical art, and false wisdom and is lord over guardians of the flame. Acts 19:19 while many of those who had practiced magic collected their books and burned them in front of everyone.

7. The kalami kingdom of the air - this kingdom is the highest of all occultic kingdoms and is ruled by Satan himself. 2 Corinthians 4:4 the god of this age has blinded the minds of the unbelievers so they cannot

see the light of the gospel of the glory of Christ, who is the image of God.

BIBLE DOCTRINE

Five Levels Satanic Of Authority

These levels of authority are known as seals of the universe, which can be attained through a process of occultic ceremonies.

1. Cosmic seal of Devic # 333. This level of authority opens direct connection with satan, releasing demonic instructions.

2. Cosmic Seal of Kal # 666. This level of authority controls leaders, politicians, military commanders, etc. This will be the occult level of the coming Antichrist.

3. Cosmic Seal of Shiva # 999. Authority to bring chaos, destruction and death.

4. Cosmic Seal of Ba-Vara # 1330. This demonic seal is known as the terrestrial seal and given to Grand Master of the Order of Astral and Terrestrial Hierarchy.

5. Cosmic Seal of Tuzassotama # 003. The one who has received this cosmic seal is mystically empowered to proclaim himself as "God, Lord, Universal Master or God-Incarnate" on earth and he controls all spirits of the occult kingdoms.

The Personality Of Satan:

1. Satan is real and is not a creature of flesh and blood. 1 Corinthians 15: 40 There are heavenly bodies and earthly bodies, but the splendor of

the heavenly bodies is different from that of the earthly ones.

2. Satan possesses intelligence. 2 Corinthians 11:3 But I fear that, as the serpent deceived Eve by his cunning, your minds may be seduced from a complete and pure devotion to Christ.

3. Satan possesses a will. 2 Timothy 2:26 Then they may come to their senses and escape the Devil's trap, having been captured by him to do his will.

4. Satan possesses a memory and thought. Matthew 4: 1-11 Then Jesus was led up by the Spirit into the wilderness to be tempted by the Devil. After He had fasted 40 days and 40 nights, He was hungry. Then the tempter approached Him and said, "If You are the Son of God, tell these stones to become bread." But He answered, "It is written: Man must not live on bread alone but on every word that comes from the mouth of God." Then the Devil took Him to the holy city, had Him stand on the pinnacle of the temple, and said to Him, "If You are the Son of God, throw Yourself down. For it is written: He will give His angels orders concerning you, and they will support you with their hands so that you will not strike your foot against a stone." Jesus told him, "It is also written: Do not test the Lord your God." Again, the Devil took Him to a very high mountain and showed Him all the kingdoms of the world and their splendor. And he said to Him, "I will give You all these things if You will fall down and worship me." Then Jesus told him, "Go away, Satan! For it is written: Worship the Lord your God, and serve only Him." Then the Devil left Him, and immediately angels came and began

BIBLE DOCTRINE

to serve Him.

5. Satan possesses organizational skills. Revelation 12;4 It was Satan who used great skill and tactics to deceive one-third of all the angles to go against God.

6. Satan possesses emotions.

    a. Desire. Luke 22: 31 Simon, Simon, look out! Satan has asked to sift you like wheat.

    b. Pride. 1 Timothy 3:6 He must not be a new convert, or he might become conceited and fall into the condemnation of the Devil.

    c. Wrath. Revelation 12:12 Woe to the earth and the sea,

    d. for the Devil has come down to you

    e. with great fury,

    f. because he knows he has a short time.

The Names And Titles Of Lucifer: Isaiah 14:12

The names and titles of satan, reveal his true perverted evil character.

1. Adversary. Used 52 times in scripture.

2. Anointed Cherub. Ezekiel 28:14 You were an anointed guardian cherub,...

3. Angel of the Abyss. Revelation 9:11 They had as their king the angel of the abyss; his name in Hebrew is Abaddon,

4. Accuser of brethren. Revelation 12:10 ...because the accuser of our brothers has been thrown out: the one who accuses them before our God, day and night.

5. Apollyon. Revelation 9:11 ... and in Greek he has the name Apollyon.

6. Angel of light. 2 Corinthians 11:14,15 For Satan disguises himself as an angel of light. So it is no great thing if his servants also disguise themselves as servants of righteousness. Their destiny will be according to their works.

7. Beelzebub. Matthew 12:24 The man drives out demons only by Beelzebul, the ruler of the demons.

8. Belial. 2 Corinthians 6:15 w hat agreement does Christ have with Belial?

9. Dragon. Revelation 12:7 Michael and his angels fought against the dragon. The dragon and his angels also fought

10. Deceiver. Revelation 20:10 The Devil who deceived them.

11. Daystar and destroyer. Isaiah 14:12 Shining morning star, how you have fallen from the heavens! You destroyer of nations,

12. Father of Lies. John 8:44 You are of your father the lies,

13. God of this age. 2 Corinthians 4:4 the god of this age has blinded the minds of the unbelievers so they cannot see the light of the gospel of the glory of Christ,

14. King of death. Hebrews 2:14 ... so that through His death He might destroy the one holding the power of death — that is, the Devil...

15. Leviathan. Isaiah 27:1 On that day the LORD with His harsh, great, and strong sword, will bring judgment on Leviathan, the fleeing serpent — Leviathan, the twisting serpent. He will slay the monster that is in the sea.
16. Lying spirit. 1 Kings 22:22 I will go and become a lying spirit in the mouth of all his prophets...
17. Like a roaring lion. 1 Peter 5:8 ... Your adversary the Devil is prowling around like a roaring lion, looking for anyone he can devour.
18. Murderer. John 8:44 ... He was a murderer from the beginning and has not stood in the truth,...
19. Prince of this world. John 12:31 ... Now the ruler of this world will be cast out.
20. Prince of the power of the air. Ephesians 2:2 in which you previously walked according to the ways of this world, according to the ruler who exercises authority over the lower heavens, the spirit now working in the disobedient.
21. Ruler of darkness. Ephesians 6:12 For we do not wrestle against flesh and blood, but against principalities, against powers, against the rulers of the darkness of this age, against spiritual hosts of wickedness in the heavenly places.
22. Ruler of demons. Matthew 9:34 He casts out demons by the ruler of the demons.

23. Satan / Adversary is used 52 times in scripture. 1 Peter 5:8 Be sober, be vigilant; because your adversary the devil walks about like a roaring lion, seeking whom he may devour.

24. Slanderer is used 35 times in the Bible. Job 2:3,4 ...although you incited Me against him, to destroy him without cause."

    So Satan answered the LORD and said, "Skin for skin! Yes, all that a man has he will give for his life.

    In the Septuagint, the Hebrew word ha-Satan is translated by the Greek word diabolos which is slanderer and the same word in the Greek New Testament is the word devi.

25. Spirit of infirmity. Luke 13:12 Woman, you are loosed from your infirmity.

26. Spirit of fear. 2 Timothy 1:7 For God has not given us a spirit of fear, but of power and of love and of a sound mind.

27. Familiar spirits. 1 Samuel 28:7 Find me a woman who is a medium, that I may go to her and inquire of her. And his servants said to him, In fact, there is a woman who is a medium at En Dor.

28. Spirit of Divination. Acts 16:16 Now it happened, as we went to prayer, that a certain slave girl possessed with a spirit of divination met us, who brought her masters much profit by fortune-telling.

29. Seducing Spirits. 1 Timothy 4:1 Now the Spirit expressly says that in latter times some will depart from the faith, giving heed to deceiving spirits and doctrines of demons,

30. Spirit of Jealousy. Genesis 4:6,7 Why are you angry? And why has your countenance fallen? If you do well, will you not be accepted? And if you do not do well, sin lies at the door. And its desire is for you, but you should rule over it.

31. Spirit of Haughtiness. 1 Samuel 15:23 For rebellion is as the sin of witchcraft, and stubbornness is as iniquity and idolatry. Because you have rejected the word of the LORD, He also has rejected you from being king.

32. Spirit of Heaviness. Isaiah 61:3 To console those who mourn in Zion, to give them beauty for ashes, The oil of joy for mourning, The garment of praise for the spirit of heaviness; That they may be called trees of righteousness, The planting of the LORD, that He may be glorified."

33. Spirit of Whoredom. Ezekiel 16:15 But you trusted in your own beauty, played the harlot because of your fame, and poured out your harlotry on everyone passing by who would have it.

34. Deaf and Dumb Spirit. Matthew 9:32 As they went out, behold, they brought to Him a man, mute and demon-possessed.

35. Spirit of Bondage. Romans 6:16 Do you not know that to whom you present yourselves slaves to obey, you are that one's slaves whom you obey, whether of sin leading to death, or of obedience leading to righteousness?

36. Spirit of Anti-Christ. 1 John 2:18 Little children, it is the last hour; and as you have heard that the Antichrist is coming, even now many antichrists have come, by which we know that it is the last hour.

37. Spirit of Error. Proverbs 14:22 Do they not go astray who devise evil? ut mercy and truth belong to those who devise good.
38. Spirit of death, poverty, and belial the destroyer. Psalm 18:4 The pangs of death surrounded me, And the floods of ungodliness made me afraid.
39. The devil. Matthew 4:1 Then Jesus was led up by the Spirit into the wilderness to be tempted by the devil.
40. The enemy. Matthew. 13:39 The enemy who sowed them is the devil, the harvest is the end of the age, and the reapers are the angels.
41. The evil one. Matthew 13:19 When anyone hears the word of the kingdom, and does not understand it, then the evil one comes and snatches away what was sown in his heart. This is he who received seed by the wayside.
42. Tempter. 1 Thessalonians. 3:5 For this reason, when I could no longer endure it, I sent to know your faith, lest by some means the tempter had tempted you, and our labor might be in vain.
43. Unclean spirit and perverse spirit; Mark 5:8, Exodus 20:13
44. Wicked one. 1 John 5:19 We know that we are of God, and the whole world lies under the sway of the wicked one.

The Activities Of Satan.

1. His primary activity is to steal, kill, and destroy. John 10:10 A thief comes only to steal and to kill and to destroy.

2. He is the great imitator. 2 Corinthians 11:14 For Satan disguises himself as an angel of light.
3. He demands worship. Revelation 13:4 They worshiped the dragon because he gave authority to the beast.
4. He instigates false doctrines. 1 Timothy 4:1 Now the Spirit explicitly says that in later times some will depart from the faith, paying attention to deceitful spirits and the teachings of demons,
5. He has his fallen angels who work for him. Revelation 12:7 Then war broke out in heaven: Michael and his angels fought against the dragon. The dragon and his angels also fought,
6. He demands sacrifices. 1 Corinthians 10:20 No, but I do say that what they sacrifice, they sacrifice to demons and not to God.
7. He sows discord among God's children. Matthew. 13:27,28 Then where did the weeds come from?' " 'An enemy did this!'
8. He hinders the work of God's servants. 1 Thessalonians 2:2 after we had previously suffered, and we were treated outrageously in Philippi, as you know, we were emboldened by our God to speak the gospel of God to you in spite of great opposition
9. He resists the prayers of God's children. Daniel 10:13 But the prince of the kingdom of Persia opposed me for 21 days. Then Michael, one of the chief princes, came to help me after I had been left there with the kings of Persia.
10. He blinds people from the Truth. 2 Corinthians 4:4 In their case, the god of this age has blinded the minds of the unbelievers so they cannot

see the light of the gospel of the glory of Christ, who is the image of God.

11. He steals The Word of God from your heart. Matthew 13:19 When anyone hears the word about the kingdom and doesn't understand it, the evil one comes and snatches away what was sown in his heart. This is the one sown along the path.

12. He accuser's believers God. Job 1:7-12 Haven't You placed a hedge around him, his household, and everything he owns? You have blessed the work of his hands, and his possessions have increased in the land. But stretch out Your hand and strike everything he owns, and he will surely curse You to Your face." "Very well," the LORD told Satan, "everything he owns is in your power. However, you must not lay a hand on Job himself." So Satan left the LORD'S presence.

13. He lays snares. 2 Timothy 2:26 Then they may come to their senses and escape the Devil's trap, having been captured by him to do his will.

14. He tempts. Matthew. 4:1 Then Jesus was led up by the Spirit into the wilderness to be tempted by the Devil.

15. He afflicts. Job 2:7 So Satan left the LORD'S presence and infected Job with terrible boils from the sole of his foot to the top of his head.

Weapons Of Satan

1. Flaming arrows of the evil one. Ephesians 6:16 In every situation take the shield of faith, and with it you will be able to extinguish all the

flaming arrows of the evil one.

2. Flaming arrows of lies. John 8:44 You are of your father the devil, and your will is to do your father's desires.

3. Flaming arrows of accusation. Matthew 10:11 Blessed are you when they revile and persecute you, and say all kinds of evil against you falsely for My sake.

4. Flaming arrows of division.

5. Flaming arrows of opposition.

6. Flaming arrows of disappointment. Romans 8:28 And we know that all things work together for good to those who love God, to those who are the called according to His purpose.

7. Flaming arrows of deception. Genesis 3:13 The serpent deceived me, and I ate.

8. Flaming arrows of distraction. Mark 4:19 Then the cares and anxieties of the world and distractions of the age, and the pleasure and delight and false glamour and deceitfulness of riches, and the craving and passionate desire for other things creep in and choke and suffocate the Word, and it becomes fruitless.

9. Flaming arrows of delay. Daniel 10:12 Then he said to me, Fear not, Daniel, for from the first day that you set your mind and heart to understand and to humble yourself before your God, your words were heard, and I have come as a consequence of [and in response to] your words.

10. Flaming arrows of temptation. Matthew 4:1-3 Then Jesus was led up by the Spirit into the wilderness to be tempted by the devil. And after fasting forty days and forty nights, he was hungry. And the tempter came and said to him, "If you are the Son of God, command these stones to become loaves of bread."

11. Flaming arrows to twist scripture. Matthew 4:5-7 Then the devil took him to the holy city and set him on the pinnacle of the temple [6] and said to him, "If you are the Son of God, throw yourself down, for it is written, "'He will command his angels concerning you,' and "'On their hands they will bear you up, lest you strike your foot against a stone.'" Jesus said to him, "Again it is written, 'You shall not put the Lord your God to the test.'"

12. Flaming arrows of Doubt. Genesis 3:1 Now the serpent was more crafty than any other beast of the field that the LORD God had made. He said to the woman, "Did God actually say, 'You shall not eat of any tree in the garden'?"

13. Flaming arrows of condemnation. Romans 8:21 There is no condemnation for those in Christ Jesus.

14. Flaming arrows of pain. 1 Peter 5:8 Be sober-minded; be watchful.

15. Flaming arrows for pleasures of the world. Deuteronomy 28:47-48 Because you did not serve the LORD your God with joyfulness and gladness of heart, because of the abundance of all things, therefore you shall serve your enemies.

16. Flaming arrows of unforgiveness. 2 Corinthians 2:10,11 Anyone whom you forgive, I also forgive. Indeed, what I have forgiven, if I have forgiven anything, has been for your sake in the presence of Christ, so that we would not be outwitted by Satan; for we are not ignorant of his designs.

17. Flaming arrows of Arrows of fear. Psalm 23:4 Even though I walk through the valley of the shadow of death, I will fear no evil, for you are with me;

BIBLE DOCTRINE

DOCTRINE OF SIN

The understanding of the doctrine of sin is most important as it is at the heart of what is wrong in our world today. It is sin that separates us from God, causes conflict between people, cripples people and families, harms society and the environment.

The word sin is found hundreds of times throughout the Old and New Testament.

There are two types of sin, accidental and deliberate.

An example of accidental sin is when you are traveling from one place to another place and you accidentally take the wrong turn and get lost, be that literal or figurative. The Hebrew word for lost in this circumstance is Rasha. To correct yourself and get back on the right path is relatively easy. Acknowledge the mistake, locate your co-ordinates, and move towards the planned destination and purposed outcome. This was a "mistake" (accidentally missing the mark), but not deliberate. Once you are back on the right path, all is well.

An example of deliberate sin is to decide and act without purpose, contrary to the plans of God. This is a deliberate act and a purposeful mistake, known as missing the mark on purpose.

BIBLE DOCTRINE

Source Of The Sin Nature

The question of the origin of sin holds importance because it tells us of a lack, a deficiency, a falling short of the standard of God's perfect goodness. All sin, no matter how trivial it may seem, falls short of the highest standard of moral perfection that is found only within God Himself.

The first man, Adam, sinned, and his transgression spiraled mankind into being born into sin and destined to live and die in sin, but God,

The second is Jesus Christ and He is the author of salvation. Hebrews 5:9 And having been perfected, He became the author of eternal salvation to all who obey Him.

Satan is the arch-enemy to Christ and satan is the author/source of sin. Satan, which means adversary, also known as the Devil. Revelation 12:9 So the great dragon was cast out, that serpent of old, called the Devil and Satan, who deceives the whole world; he was cast to the earth, and his angels were cast out with him.

Satan is the one who has been sinning from the beginning 1 John 3:8 He who sins is of the devil, for the devil has sinned from the beginning. For this purpose the Son of God was manifested, that He might destroy the works of the devil.

God extends no forgiveness/redemption to the devil and his angels who know exactly where they are headed. Matthew 8:28,29 When He had come to the other side, to the country of the Gergesenes, there met Him two demon-possessed men, coming out of the tombs, exceedingly fierce, so that no one could pass that way. And suddenly they cried out, saying, "What have we to do with You, Jesus, You Son of God? Have You come here to torment us before the time?"

The devil has one goal in mind which is to deceive the world which lies under his influence, Revelation 12:9 So the great dragon was cast out, that serpent of old, called the Devil and Satan, who deceives the whole world; he was cast to the earth, and his angels were cast out with him.

It is his desire to take the souls of mankind to hell with him. Remember what Jesus said to Peter, Luke 22:31 "Simon, Simon, behold, Satan hath desired to have you, that he may sift you as wheat".

Satan orchestrated the first sin on earth and encouraged the greatest sin against Jesus. 2 Corinthians 11:3,4 But I fear, lest somehow, as the serpent deceived Eve by his craftiness, so your minds may be corrupted from the simplicity that is in Christ. For if he who comes preaches another Jesus whom we have not preached, or if you receive a different spirit which you have not received, or a different gospel which you have not accepted—you may well put up with it!

Satan was responsible for the first sin in the church, with Ananias and Saphira, Satan "the tempter" even tried to get Jesus to sin.

Acts 5:1-4 But a certain man named Ananias, with Sapphira his wife, sold a possession. And he kept back part of the proceeds, his wife also being aware of it, and brought a certain part and laid it at the apostles' feet. But Peter said, "Ananias, why has Satan filled your heart to lie to the Holy Spirit and keep back part of the price of the land for yourself? While it remained, was it not your own? And after it was sold, was it not in your own control? Why have you conceived this thing in your heart? You have not lied to men but to God."

Matthew 4:1 Then Jesus was led up by the Spirit into the wilderness to be tempted by the devil.

Satan had no regard for God's Son, or for you and he will do everything he can to draw you away from God.

James 1:14,15 But each one is tempted when he is drawn away by his own desires and enticed. Then, when desire has conceived, it gives birth to sin; and sin, when it is full-grown, brings forth death.

Satan will never stop transferring the blame of sin to mankind and trying to take mankind to eternal damnation with him. The only solution to successfully combating sin is to submit to God.

To the degree a person submits to God, to that same degree will the same person be able to resist satan. James 4:7 Therefore submit to God. Resist the devil and he will flee from you.

The same thing that tripped satan up in the beginning, is what satan uses against mankind to be separated from God. It is pride. The acronym for pride is best seen in the five "I wills" of satan as found in Isaiah 14:13,14 For you have said in your heart: I will ascend into heaven, I will exalt my throne above the stars of God; I will also sit on the mount of the congregation On the farthest sides of the north; I will ascend above the heights of the clouds, I will be like the Most High.'

1. I will ascend into Heaven. Lucifer wanted to occupy the highest heavens: to probe, and to penetrate the kingdom of the infinite God. He wanted to have a very HIGH position!
2. I will exalt my throne above the stars of God. Lucifer's position and service before God's throne was not enough. He wanted a throne from which he could exercise final authority and make decisions pertaining to the angelic host.
3. I will sit also upon the mount of the congregation. Lucifer wanted to be the center of attention. He wanted to be idolized by all.
4. I will ascend above the heights of the clouds. Lucifer wanted God's dazzling glory for his own.

5. I will be like the Most-High. Lucifer wanted to be equal with God and to take God's place as the possessor and ruler of all.

The Hebrew Words For Sin Are:

1. Hhatah literally means "miss the mark."
2. Râ âh means evil, bad, and contrary to the nature of God.
3. Cha â'âh is translated as an offense deserving of punishment.
4. Râshâ is most often translated as wicked and morally wrong.
5. Âvôn is translated iniquity, perverse, crooked, and twisted.
6. Pesha is translated transgression and rebellion.
7. 'Âsham is translated as guilty of offense or trespass.
8. Tâ Âh is translated to go astray, deceive, dissemble, err, pant, seduce, (make to) stagger, (cause to) wander, be out of the way.
9. Pâsha is translated to break away from just authority, to trespass, apostatize, quarrel: - offend, rebel, revolt, and to transgress.
10. Shâgâh is translated to stray, to mistake, to transgress, to be deceive, to err, to be ravished, to sin through ignorance, and to wander.

The Greek Words For Sin Are:

1. Hamartia is translated to commit offence and sin.

2. Parapt ma is translated to unintentionally error transgress, to fall, faulter, and trespass.
3. Parabasis is translated to violate and overstep a forbidden line, to transgress.
4. Asebeia is translated to impiety by wickedness.
5. Hamart ma is translated to properly sin.
6. PonRos is translated to derelict, vicious, facinorous; mischief, malice, evil, grievous, harm, lewd, malicious, wicked.
7. Kakos is translated to depraved, bad, evil, harm, ill, noisome, and wicked.
8. Adikos is translated to wicked; by implication treacherous; specifically heathen: - unjust, unrighteous.
9. Anomos is translated to without law, lawless, transgressor, unlawful, and wicked.
10. Hamartan is translated to trespass.
11. Plana is translated to go astray, deceive, err, seduce, wander, be out of the way.
12. Parabain is translated to go contrary, to violate a command, and to transgress.

Eight Metaphors Of Sin

1. Sin is poisonous, like a viper. Psalms 140:3 They make their tongues as sharp as a snake's bite; viper's venom is under their lips. Selah

2. Sin is stubborn, like a mule. Job 11:12 But a stupid man will gain understanding as soon as a wild donkey is born a man!

3. Sin is cruel, like a bear. Daniel 7:5 Suddenly, another beast appeared, a second one, that looked like a bear. It was raised up on one side, with three ribs in its mouth between its teeth. It was told, 'Get up! Gorge yourself on flesh.

4. Sin is destructive, like a locust and cankerworm. Joel 2:25 I will repay you for the years that the swarming locust ate, the young locust, the destroying locust, and the devouring locust.

5. Sin is coming, like a fox. Luke 13:32 Go tell that fox, 'Look! I'm driving out demons and performing healings today and tomorrow, and on the third day I will complete My work.'

6. Sin fierce, like a wolf. John 10:12 The hired man, since he is not the shepherd and doesn't own the sheep, leaves them and runs away when he sees a wolf coming. The wolf then snatches and scatters them.

7. Sin devours, like a lion. Psalms 22:13 They open their mouths against me — lions, mauling and roaring.

8. Sin is filthy, like a pig and a dog. 2 Peter 2:22 A dog returns to its own vomit, and, "a sow, after washing itself, wallows in the mud."

The Consequences Of Sin

The Bible is clear that there are negative effects and negative consequences for sins.

Romans 1:18 The wrath of God is being revealed from heaven against all the godlessness and wickedness of people, who suppress the truth by their wickedness.

Ultimately, sin leads to a final judgment where individuals are held accountable for their actions, unless they find redemption through faith in Christ.

Ten consequences of sin:

1. Death: Romans 6:23 For the wages of sin is death, but the gift of God is eternal life in Christ Jesus our Lord."
2. Separation from God: Isaiah 59:2 Your sins have separated you from your God; your sins have hidden his face from you, so that he will not hear.
3. The loss of spiritual sight: 2 Corinthians 4:4 The god of this age has blinded the minds of unbelievers, so that they cannot see the light of the gospel that displays the glory of Christ, who is the image of God.
4. Bondage to Sin: John 8:34 Jesus replied, Very truly I tell you, everyone who sins is a slave to sin.

5. The loss of joy. Psalms 51:12 Restore the joy of Your salvation to me and give me a willing spirit

6. The loss of confidence. 1 John 3:19-22 This is how we will know we belong to the truth and will convince our conscience in His presence, even if our conscience condemns us, that God is greater than our conscience, and He knows all things.

7. The loss of health and life. 1 Corinthians 11:30 This is why many are sick and ill among you, and many have fallen asleep.

8. Conscience and Guilt: Romans 2:15 They show that the requirements of the law are written on their hearts, their consciences also bearing witness, and their thoughts sometimes accusing them and at other times even defending them.

9. Broken Relationships: Proverbs 17:9 Whoever would foster love covers over an offense, but whoever repeats the matter separates close friends.

10. Suffering and Consequences: Galatians 6:7,8 Do not be deceived: God cannot be mocked. A man reaps what he sows. Whoever sows to please their flesh, from the flesh will reap destruction; whoever sows to please the Spirit, from the Spirit will reap eternal life."

The Unpardonable Sin And Sin Unto Death

The unpardonable sin is to deliberately repudiate the truth about Jesus and continually reject the convictions of the Holy Spirit.

God responds to such rebellion by hardening the rebel's heart and not giving that person a desire to repent and believe. The sin is unforgivable because God never enables that person to repent and believe.

This is a sin that only unbelievers can commit and only God knows who is guilty of this sin.

'Augustine argued that the unforgivable sin is total and final unbelief—that is, if a person persists to the end of his life in rejecting Christ, he will not receive a second chance in heaven. Such unbelief is ultimately and permanently unforgivable.'

The unpardonable sin can overlap with apostasy.

Apostasy is decisively turning away from the faith. An apostate is a person who once claimed to be a Christian but has irreversibly abandoned and renounced orthodox Christianity.

Those who commit the unpardonable sin are similar to apostates in that they have resolutely rejected the truth and are beyond repentance.

The fate of those who commit the unpardonable sin parallels the fate of apostates in at least three passages on apostasy:

Matthew 12:30-32 Anyone who is not with Me is against Me, and anyone who does not gather with Me scatters. Because of this, I tell you, people will be forgiven every sin and blasphemy, but the blasphemy against the Spirit will not be forgiven. Whoever speaks a word against the Son of Man, it will be forgiven him. But whoever speaks against the Holy Spirit, it will not be forgiven him, either in this age or in the one to come.

Mark 3:22-30 and the scribes who came down from Jerusalem said, who came down from Jerusalem said, he has beelzebub and by the ruler of Demons he cast out Demons. …. Surely, I say to you, all sins will be forgiven as sons of men, and whatever blasphemes play my answer, but he blasphemed against the Holy Spirit never has forgiven us, that is subject to eternal condemnation,…

Hebrews 6:4 For it is impossible to renew to repentance those who were once enlightened, who tasted the heavenly gift, became companions with the Holy Spirit,

Hebrews 10:29 How much worse punishment do you think one will deserve who has trampled on the Son of God, regarded as profane the blood of the covenant by which he was sanctified, and insulted the Spirit of grace?

1 John 5:16 If anyone sees his brother committing a sin that does not bring death, he should ask, and God will give life to him — to those who commit sin that doesn't bring death. There is sin that brings death. I am not saying he should pray about that.

Sin unto death is mentioned as early as Genesis 2:17 but you must not eat from the tree of the knowledge of good and evil, for on the day you eat from it, you will certainly die.

BIBLE DOCTRINE

Sin unto death is a deliberate refusal to believe in the Lordship of Jesus Christ, to follow God's commands, and to love one's brothers.

Two types of death:

1. Physical Death. Ecclesiastes 12:7 … the dust returns to the earth as it once was, and the spirit returns to God who gave it. ….

    Physical death separates the spirit and soul from the body.

    When a true believer in Christ Jesus dies, immediately their soul and spirit are in the presence of the Lord, and their flesh will go into the ground.

    2 Corinthians 5:6-8 So, we are always confident and know that while we are at home in the body we are away from the Lord. For we walk by faith, not by sight, and we are confident and satisfied to be out of the body and at home with the Lord.

    When the unbeliever flesh, their flesh goes into the ground, but immediately their soul and spirit go to hell (I.e. Hades – the place of departed spirits – place of torment.

    Physical Death for the believer is not a tragedy, but a distinct glory.

2. Spiritual death. Ephesians 2:1 "and you hath He made alive, who were dead in trespasses and sins".

When a non-believer dies, their body goes into the ground at burial, while their spirit and soul go directly to hell, where they are separated from God for eternity.

Romans 6:23 declares that the "wages of sin is death" (i.e. spiritual death and, of course, this includes physical death).

BIBLE DOCTRINE

DOCTRINE OF HEAVEN AND HELL

Doctrine Of Heaven

Deuteronomy 10:14 The heavens, indeed the highest heavens, belong to the LORD your God, as does the earth and everything in it.

The word heaven means lofty or elevation.

Heaven is used in the Bible 551 times, 313 times in the Old Testament, and 238 times in the New Testament.

Consider that hell is mentioned only 54 times in the Bible.

The Bible speaks of Heaven ten times more than hell.

The heavens were made by God, the Son, and The Holy Spirit

1. Genesis 1:1 In the beginning God created the heaven and the earth.
2. Job 26: 13, "By His spirit he hath garnished the heavens; his hand hath formed the crooked serpent."
3. Psalm 33:6 By the Word of the Lord, were the heavens made; and all the host of them by the breath of his mouth.

BIBLE DOCTRINE

The Three Heavens

2 Corinthians 12:2 I know a man in Christ who was caught up into the third heaven 14 years ago. Whether he was in the body or out of the body, I don't know, God knows.

1. The First Heaven / Atmospheric Heaven

The first Heaven is the atmospheric heaven is the space surrounding the earth and extending to a height of about 6 miles and is called the tropospher.

The word first as in first Heaven is found seven times in the first chapter of the Bible and Twenty-one times throughout the Bible.

One example is when Jesus speaks of the first Heaven in Matthew 8:20 'And Jesus saith unto him The foxes have holes, and the birds of the air have nests; but the Son of man hath not where to lay his head.'

2. The Second Heaven / Celestial Heaven

The second heaven is the region we call outer space, the realm of the sun, moon, stars, and planets, galaxies, black holes, etc.

Genesis 1:1 In the beginning God created the heavens and the earth.

Genesis 1:14-17 Then God said, let there be lights in the expanse of the heavens to separate the day from the night, and let them be for signs and for seasons and for days and **years and** let them be for lights in the expanse of the heavens to give light on the earth and it was so. God made the two great lights, the greater light to govern the day, and the lesser light to govern the night; He made the stars also. God placed them in the expanse of the heavens to give light on the earth

The phrase "stars of heaven" occurs eleven times in scripture. Genesis 1:14-17, "And God said, let there be lights in the firmament of the heaven to divide the day from the night; and let them be for signs, and for seasons, and for days, and years: And let them be for lights in the firmament of the heaven to give light upon the earth: and it was so. And God made two great lights; the greater light to rule the day, and the lesser light to rule the night: he made the stars also. And God set them in the firmament of the heaven to give light upon the earth," This is speaking of our sun and our moon.

3. The Third Heaven / Dwelling Place of God

The first two heavens will pass away, but the third heaven is eternal. The third Heaven is also known as the courts of Heaven and the place where God's presence dwells.

Matthew 6:9 Our Father in heaven, Your Name be honored as holy.

Paul referred to the third heaven in 2 Corinthians 12:2 I know a man in Christ who was caught up into the third heaven...

1. John was taken up to the third heaven and given a glimpse of God's dwelling place in Revelation 4:1,2 After this I looked, and there in heaven was an open door. The first voice that I had heard speaking to me like a trumpet said, "Come up here, and I will show you what must

take place after this. Immediately I was in the Spirit, and a throne was set there in heaven. One was seated on the throne,

God sits enthroned in the third heaven as seen in Psalm 2:4 He who sits in the heavens laughs, The Lord scoffs at them.

The third heaven is called Paradise in Luke 23:43, And Jesus said unto him, Verily I say unto thee, To day shalt thou be with me in paradise.

The New Jerusalem

Revelation 21 and 22

Ten points to consider concerning the New Jerusalem.

1. The New Jerusalem is the Bride of Christ and the Wife of the Lamb.
2. The New Jerusalem is radiant with beauty, opulence, glory, splendor, and sanctification.
3. The New Jerusalem has the river of Life from through her that produces fruit all year round.
4. The New Jerusalem is the depiction of a city, heavenly in nature, blessed with the glory of God himself, surrounded by a huge wall, reflecting absolute security.
5. The New Jerusalem has 12 gates which are 12 pearls. The gates of the city never ever close, as there is no threat as Heaven's enemies have been eternally dealt with.

6. On the gates of the New Jerusalem are written the names of the tribes of Israel and the wall is undergirded by twelve foundations upon which are the names of the twelve apostles.

7. The New Jerusalem is 12,000 stadia, which is an area of(1,500 miles in each direction of width, breadth, and height.

8. The New Jerusalem is reminiscent of the Holy of Holies in the tabernacle, with unparalleled beauty and value portrayed by pure gold and brilliant gems.

9. The building material for the walls of the New Jerusalem iss jasper, and city itself is pure gold like clear glass.

10. In The New Jerusalem, there is no natural light for the glory of God and the Lamb is the Light.

The Words Of Jesus Concerning Heaven

Jesus spoke more about eternal life and how one can enter Heaven than He did about Heaven itself. The words of Jesus concerning Heaven reveal to us some of the secrets that are still to be revealed.

Below are the words of Jesus recorded by Matthew, Mark, Luke, and John.

The Book of Matthew

Matthew 5:12 Rejoice, and be exceeding glad: for great *is* your reward in heaven...

Matthew 5:16 Let your light so shine before men, that they may see your good works and glorify your Father in heaven.

Matthew 5:45 that you may be sons of your Father in heaven; for He makes His sun rise on the evil and on the good, and sends rain on the just and on the unjust.

Matthew 5:48 Therefore you shall be perfect, just as your Father in heaven is perfect.

Matthew 6:1 Take heed that you do not do your charitable deeds before men, to be seen by them. Otherwise you have no reward from your Father in heaven.

Matthew 6:9 In this manner, therefore, pray: Our Father in heaven, Hallowed be Your name.

Matthew 6:19,20 Do not lay up for yourselves treasures on earth, where moth and rust destroy and where thieves break in and steal but lay up for yourselves treasures in heaven, where neither moth nor rust destroys and where thieves do not break in and steal.

Matthew 7:11 If you then, being evil, know how to give good gifts to your children, how much more will your Father who is in heaven give good things to those who ask Him!

Matthew 7:21 Not everyone who says to Me, 'Lord, Lord,' shall enter the kingdom of heaven, but he who does the will of My Father in heaven.

Matthew 10:32,33 Therefore whoever confesses Me before men, him I will also confess before My Father who is in heaven. But whoever denies Me before men, him I will also deny before My Father who is in heaven.

Matthew 11:25 I thank thee, O Father, Lord of heaven and earth...

Matthew 12:50 For whoever does the will of My Father in heaven is My brother and sister and mother.

Matthew 16:17 Jesus answered and said to him, "Blessed are you, Simon Bar-Jonah, for flesh and blood has not revealed this to you, but My Father who is in heaven.

Matthew 18: 10 Take heed that you do not despise one of these little ones, for I say to you that in heaven their angels always see the face of My Father who is in heaven.

Matthew 18:14 Even so it is not the will of your Father who is in heaven that one of these little ones should perish.

Matthew 18:19 Again I say to you that if two of you agree on earth concerning anything that they ask, it will be done for them by My Father in heaven.

Matthew 23:9 Do not call anyone on earth your father; for One is your Father, He who is in heaven.

The Book of Mark

Mark 11:25, 26 And whenever you stand praying, if you have anything against anyone, forgive him, that your Father in heaven may also forgive you your trespasses. But if you do not forgive, neither will your Father in heaven forgive your trespasses.

Mark 13:32 But of that day and hour no one knows, not even the angels in heaven, nor the Son, but only the Father.

The Book of Luke

Luke 6:23 Rejoice in that day and leap for joy! For indeed your reward *is* great in heaven...

Luke 10:21 I thank thee, O Father, Lord of heaven and earth...

Luke 11:22 So He said to them, When you pray, say: Our Father in heaven, Hallowed be Your name. Your kingdom come. Your will be done On earth as it is in heaven.

Luke 15:7 I say to you that likewise there will be more joy in heaven over one sinner who repents than over ninety-nine just persons who need no repentance.

The Book of John

John 14:2-4 In My Father's house are many dwelling places; if not, I would have told you. I am going away to prepare a place for you. If I go away and prepare a place for you, I will come back and receive you to Myself, so that where I am you may be also. You know the way to where I am going."

BIBLE DOCTRINE

Doctrine Of Hell

Jesus spoke more about hell than anyone else in all the Bible.

There are thirty-one different passages in the Gospels where Jesus speaks of hell.

Amazingly 13% of his sayings are about hell and judgment, and more than half of His parables relate to the eternal judgment of sinners.

The Three Hells

1. Gehenna is also called the lake of fire and is the final place of punishment for all who reject God's plan of salvation. Revelation 20:10 The Devil who deceived them was thrown into the lake of fire and sulfur where the beast and the false prophet are, ...
2. Hades also known as Sheol is the final destiny of all who reject God, Hades is the present place of imprisonment for the disembodied spirits of lost humans.

    Luke 16:19-31 The rich man also died and was buried. And being in torment in Hades, he lifted up his eyes and saw Abraham afar off, and Lazarus in his bosom.

    The easiest to describe Hades and Gehenna is, Hades is the "county jail" (temporary prison) and Gehenna is the "penitentiary" (eternal prison).

3. Tartarus is the bottomless pit, called the abyss. Tartarus / the Abyss is a place where the fallen angels from Genesis 6 are being held, and in 2 Peter 2:4 For if God didn't spare the angels who sinned but threw them down into Tartarus and delivered them to be kept in chains of darkness until judgment;

The abyss appears 9 times in the New Testament.

1) Luke 8:31 And they begged Him not to banish them to the abyss.
2) Romans 10:7 "Who will go down into the abyss?"
3) Revelation 9:1,2 The fifth angel blew his trumpet, and I saw a star that had fallen from heaven to earth. The key to the shaft of the abyss was given to him. He opened the shaft of the abyss, and smoke came up out of the shaft like smoke from a great furnace so that the sun and the air were darkened by the smoke from the shaft.
4) Revelation 9:11 They had as their king the angel of the abyss; his name in Hebrew is Abaddon, and in Greek he has the name Apollyon.
5) Revelation 11:7 When they finish their testimony, the beast that comes up out of the abyss will make war with them, conquer them, and kill them.
6) Revelation 20:1 Then I saw an angel coming down from heaven with the key to the abyss and a great chain in his hand.
7) Revelation 20:3 He threw him into the abyss, closed it, and put a seal on it so that he would no longer deceive the nations until the

1,000 years were completed. After that, he must be released for a short time.

8) The legion of demons in the Gadarene demoniac begged Jesus to go into some pigs. They also asked Him not to send them into "the abyss" before the time. Luke 8:31 And they begged Him not to banish them to the abyss.

9) The Antichrist ascends from the abyss as seen in Revelation 17:8 The beast that you saw was, and is not, and is about to come up from the abyss and go to destruction.

The Words Of Jesus About Hell and Judgment
The Book of Matthew

Matthew 5:22 But I say to you that whoever is angry with his brother without a cause shall be in danger of the judgment. And whoever says to his brother, 'Raca!' shall be in danger of the council. But whoever says, 'You fool!' shall be in danger of hellfire.

Matthew 5:29 If your right eye causes you to sin, pluck it out and cast it from you; for it is more profitable for you that one of your members perish than for your whole body to be cast into hell.

Matthew 10: 28 And do not fear those who kill the body but cannot kill the soul. But rather fear Him who is able to destroy both soul and body in hell.

Matthew 11:23 And you, Capernaum, who are exalted to heaven, will be brought down to hell; for if the mighty works which were done in you had been done in Sodom, it would have remained until this day.

Matthew 16:18 And I also say to you that you are Peter, and on this rock I will build My church, and the gates of hell shall not prevail against it.

Matthew 18:9 And if your eye causes you to sin, pluck it out and cast it from you. It is better for you to enter into life with one eye, rather than having two eyes, to be cast into hell fire.

Matthew 23:9 Woe to you, scribes and Pharisees, hypocrites! For you travel land and sea to win one proselyte, and when he is won, you make him twice as much a son of hell as yourselves.

Matthew 23:33 Serpents, brood of vipers! How can you escape the condemnation of hell?

The Gospel of Mark

In Mark, Jesus mentioned hell only three times in one passage. However, in that passage, He gave a clear message of warning of the dangers of hell and the presence of flames of fire.

Mark 9:43 If your hand causes you to sin, cut it off. It is better for you to enter into life maimed, rather than having two hands, to go to hell, into the fire that shall never be quenched.

Mark 9:45 And if your foot causes you to sin, cut it off. It is better for you to enter life lame, rather than having two feet, to be cast into hell, into the fire that shall never be quenched.

Mark 9:47 And if your eye causes you to sin, pluck it out. It is better for you to enter the kingdom of God with one eye, rather than having two eyes, to be cast into hell fire.

The Gospel of Luke

Luke 10:15 And you, Capernaum, who are exalted to heaven, will be brought down to hell.

Luke 12:5 But I will show you whom you should fear: Fear Him who, after He has killed, has power to cast into hell; yes, I say to you, fear Him!

Luke 16:23 And being in torments in hell, he lifted up his eyes and saw Abraham afar off, and Lazarus in his bosom.

Other expressions Jesus used concerning such as destruction, fire, flame, condemnation, and perishing.

Matthew 7:13 Enter by the narrow gate; for wide is the gate and broad is the way that leads to destruction, and there are many who go in by it.

Matthew 7:19 Every tree that does not bear good fruit is cut down and thrown into the fire.

Matthew 13:40 Therefore as the tares are gathered and burned in the fire, so it will be at the end of this age.

Matthew 13:42 and will cast them into the furnace of fire. There will be wailing and gnashing of teeth.

Matthew 13:50 and cast them into the furnace of fire. There will be wailing and gnashing of teeth.

BIBLE DOCTRINE

Matthew 18:8 If your hand or foot causes you to sin, cut it off and cast it from you. It is better for you to enter into life lame or maimed, rather than have two hands or two feet, to be cast into the everlasting fire.

Matthew 22:13 Then the king said to the servants, Bind him hand and foot, take him away, and cast him into outer darkness; there will be weeping and gnashing of teeth.

Matthew 25:30 And cast the unprofitable servant into the outer darkness. There will be weeping and gnashing of teeth.

Matthew 25:41 Then He will also say to those on the left hand, Depart from Me, you cursed, into the everlasting fire prepared for the devil and his angels:

Matthew 9:44, 46, 48 where Their worm does not die, And the fire is not quenched.

Mark 12:40 who devour widows' houses, and for a pretense make long prayers. These will receive greater condemnation.

Luke 13:3 I tell you, no; but unless you repent you will all likewise perish.

Luke 16:24 Then he cried and said, Father Abraham, have mercy on me, and send Lazarus that he may dip the tip of his finger in water and cool my tongue; for I am tormented in this flame.

John 5:29 and come forth; those who have done good, to the resurrection of life, and those who have done evil, to the resurrection of condemnation.

John 15:6 If anyone does not abide in Me, he is cast out as a branch and is withered; and they gather them and throw them into the fire, and they are burned.

BIBLE DOCTRINE

DOCTRINE OF THE TWO KINGDOMS

The word "kingdom" is a translation of the Greek word "basileia" which in turn is a translation of the words "malkuth" (Hebrew) and "malkutha" (Aramaic). These words do not define kingdom by territory but by dominion. Dominion originated in the heart of God and mankind was created to have dominion over all the earth.

Dominion in Hebrew is Shalat and it definition is o be the ruler, to be the master, to have power.

Dominion in Greek is Kratos and its definition is to strength and might.

Kingdom in Hebrew is Mam-lakah and its definition is kingdom, sovereign rule or royal power.

Kingdom in Greek is Basileia and its definition is Kingdom, sovereignty, royal power.

Merriam Webster definition of kingdom is the governing influence of a king over his territory in all areas of life, animal kingdom, mineral kingdom and plant kingdom.

BIBLE DOCTRINE

The Kingdom of God is the original governing system designed for earth.

There are two kingdoms according to Colossians 1;13

KINGDOM OF DARKNESS KINGDOM OF THIS WORLD KINGDOM OF SATAN		KINGDOM OF GOD KINGDOM OF HEAVEN KINGDOM OF HIS SON
Ephesians 2;2 The prince of the power of the air, the spirit that now works in the children of disobedience.		Revelation 11;15 The kingdom of this world have become the kingdoms of our God
Satan		GOD
KING	Satan	Jesus
Kingdom	World	Heaven and Earth
Citizens	Faithless	Believers
Law	Lies	Truth
Constitution	People	I The Lord
Customs	Evil	Righteousness
Power	Illusion	Victory
Destiny	Hell	Kingdom of Heaven

The kingdom of darkness is; Atheism, Secularism, Humanism, Agnosticism, Communism, Feudalism, Dictatorship, Socialism, and Democracy

FOUNDATIONS OF FAITH

The Kingdom of God is; Less of me and more the King.

The Work Of The Kingdom Of God Has 5 important tasks:

1. Kingdom focuses on Earth.
2. Kingdom is God coming down to man.
3. Kingdom impacts, influences and changes earth.
4. Kingdom seeks to bring Heaven to earth.
5. Kingdom is inter-realm transfer.

The Kingdom of God is;

Love, Joy, Peace and Righteousness in the Holy Spirit.

1. God's rule with mercy and justice practiced through the church, while submitting to God's authority.
2. The church on earth living in word and action exercising the Kingdom of God that is in Heaven on Earth.
3. The Kingdom of God is you the church living in your full restoration in all areas of life, animal kingdom, mineral kingdom and plant kingdom.

BIBLE DOCTRINE

DOCTRINE OF ESCHATOLOGY

Eschatology is the study of the last things, it is the capstone of systematic theology with every branch of theology finding finality in it.

Eschatology deals with death, the end of the world, the ultimate destiny of humankind, the final events in the history of the world, the second coming of Christ, the resurrection of the dead, the last judgment, Heaven and hell.

Eschatology is derived from two Greek words;

Eschatos	ἔστατος	last, uttermost and final.
Logos	λόγος	word, study, and reason.

The return of Jesus Christ, also called the second coming of Christ or the Advent of Christ is the central teaching in the Bible, and is found in Acts 1:11 "Men of Galilee, why do you stand looking up into heaven? This Jesus, who has been taken from you into heaven, will come in the same way that you have seen Him going into heaven."

The return of Jesus Christ will be visible and physical as He comes from heaven on the clouds to bring final judgment and salvation.
The nature of the Second Coming is visible, imminent, and final.

BIBLE DOCTRINE

The New Testament establishes the doctrine of the second coming of Jesus and refers to His return in splendor and glory, yet at the same time being dreadful for others.

The term "Second Coming of Jesus Christ' does not occur in the New Testament, though there are several nouns and verbs used to refer to the return of Christ.

Seven Categories Eschatology

1. Christ's second Coming; Titus 2:13 while we wait for the blessed hope and appearing of the glory of our great God and Savior, Jesus Christ.
2. Death; Acts 23:6 When Paul realized that one part of them were Sadducees and the other part were Pharisees, he cried out in the Sanhedrin, "Brothers, I am a Pharisee, a son of Pharisees! I am being judged because of the hope of the resurrection of the dead!"
3. Millennium; 1000yr period specified about the kingdom of God, the day of the Lord, and the reign of the Messiah. The word millennium is not found in Scripture, though its meaning is mentioned six times in Scripture. Revelation 20:2-7 He seized the dragon, that ancient serpent who is the Devil and Satan, and bound him for 1,000 years. He threw him into the abyss, closed it, and put a seal on it so that he would no longer deceive the nations until the 1,000 years were completed. After that, he must be released for a short time. Then I saw thrones, and

people seated on them who were given authority to judge. I also saw the people who had been beheaded because of their testimony about Jesus and because of God's word, who had not worshiped the beast or his image, and who had not accepted the mark on their foreheads or their hands. They came to life and reigned with the Messiah for 1,000 years. The rest of the dead did not come to life until the 1,000 years were completed. This is the first resurrection. Blessed and holy is the one who shares in the first resurrection! The second death has no power over them, but they will be priests of God and of the Messiah, and they will reign with Him for 1,000 years. When the 1,000 years are completed, Satan will be released from his prison...

There are five view points in millienialism.

1) Postmillennialists believe that the period is a figurative reference to a thousand-year period of global peace, equality, and godliness that will ensue before the 2nd coming.

2) Premillennialism believe the physical and earthly reign of Jesus on earth. However, contention exists among the exponents of this view concerning the place of the nation of Israel during this time.

3) Historic premillennialists believe many Jews will be part of the redeemed.

4) Dispensational premillennialists believe that the nation of Israel will inherit the Abrahamic promise at this time.

5) Amillennialism denies the one-thousand years of peace before or after the 2nd coming. Amillennialists estimate that 1000 years is a symbol of the spiritual reign of Jesus over the regenerated.

4. Resurrection; There are 2 types of resurrection.
   1) The resurrection unto life. At the beginning of the millennium. Righteous dead will rise. 1 Thessalonians 4:16 For the Lord Himself will descend from heaven with a shout, with the archangel's voice, and with the trumpet of God, and the dead in Christ will rise first.
   2) Resurrection unto death. John 5:39 You pore over the Scriptures because you think you have eternal life in them, yet they testify about Me.

   At the end of the millennium, the righteous living will rise.

5. Rapture; 1 Thessalonians 4:17 Then we who are still alive will be caught up together with them in the clouds to meet the Lord in the air and so we will always be with the Lord. We will meet The Lord in the clouds.

   There 3 views about the timing of the rapture.
   1) Pre-tribulation; Beginning of the seven-year tribulation.
   2) Mid- tribulation; Middle of the seven-year tribulation.
   3) Post-tribulation; End seven-year tribulation.

6. The Great Tribulation; is described as the day of the Lord.

   Isaiah 2:12 For a day belonging to the LORD of Hosts is coming against all that is proud and lofty, against all that is lifted up it will be humbled. Isaiah 13:6 Wail! For the day of the LORD is near. It will come like destruction from the Almighty.

Isaiah 13:9 Look, the day of the LORD is coming — cruel, with rage and burning anger — to make the earth a desolation and to destroy the sinners on it.

Joel 1:15 Woe because of that day! For the Day of the LORD is near and will come as devastation from the Almighty.

Amos 5:18 Woe to you who long for the Day of the LORD! What will the Day of the LORD be for you? It will be darkness and not light.

Obadiah 1:15 For the Day of the LORD is near, against all the nations. As you have done, so it will be done to you; what you deserve will return on your own head.

7. Judgment; There are 2 judgments.
   1) Great White Throne is judgment non-believers. Revelation 20:11-15 Then I saw a great white throne and One seated on it. Earth and heaven fled from His presence, and no place was found for them. I also saw the dead, the great and the small, standing before the throne, and books were opened. Another book was opened, which is the book of life, and the dead were judged according to their works by what was written in the books.
   2) Then the sea gave up its dead, and Death and Hades gave up their dead; all were judged according to their works. Death and Hades were thrown into the lake of fire. This is the second death, the lake of fire. And anyone not found written in the book of life was thrown into the lake of fire.

3) Bema Judgment Seat of Christ is the reward to the redeemed. 1 Corinthians 3:13 each one's work will become obvious, for the day will disclose it, because it will be revealed by fire; the fire will test the quality of each one's work.

The Central Teaching In The Bible Is 2nd Coming Of Jesus.

Acts 1:11 They said, "Men of Galilee, why do you stand looking up into heaven? This Jesus, who has been taken from you into heaven, will come in the same way that you have seen Him going into heaven."

The Date Of Jesus' Return Is Unknown.

Matthew 24:36, 37 Now concerning that day and hour no one knows — neither the angels in heaven, nor the Son — except the Father only. As the days of Noah were, so the coming of the Son of Man will be.

There Are Two Viewpoints Of Jesus's Return;

1. Delayed return; Kingdom now. Matthew 24:14 This good news of the kingdom will be proclaimed in all the world as a testimony to all nations. And then the end will come.
2. Eminent return; Kingdom then. Matthew 24:42-44 Therefore be alert, since you don't know what day your Lord is coming. But know this: If

the homeowner had known what time the thief was coming, he would have stayed alert and not let his house be broken into. This is why you also must be ready, because the Son of Man is coming at an hour you do not expect.

Five Ways Jesus Christ Will Return;

1. Personal, physical coming. Acts 1:11 They said, "Men of Galilee, why do you stand looking up into heaven? This Jesus, who has been taken from you into heaven, will come in the same way that you have seen Him going into heaven."

2. Visible coming. Matthew 24:27 For as the lightning comes from the east and flashes as far as the west, so will be the coming of the Son of Man.

3. Sudden. Matthew 24:37-44 As the days of Noah were, so the coming of the Son of Man will be. For in those days before the flood they were eating and drinking, marrying and giving in marriage, until the day Noah boarded the ark. They didn't know until the flood came and swept them all away. So this is the way the coming of the Son of Man will be: Then two men will be in the field: one will be taken and one left. Two women will be grinding at the mill: one will be taken and one left. Therefore be alert, since you don't know what day your Lord is coming. But know this: If the homeowner had known what time the thief was coming, he would have stayed alert and not let his house be

broken into. This is why you also must be ready, because the Son of Man is coming at an hour you do not expect.

4. Glorious. Titus 2:13 while we wait for the blessed hope and appearing of the glory of our great God and Savior, Jesus Christ.

5. Victorious. Revelation 19:11-16 Then I saw heaven opened, and there was a white horse. Its rider is called Faithful and True, and He judges and makes war in righteousness. His eyes were like a fiery flame, and many crowns were on His head. He had a name written that no one knows except Himself. He wore a robe stained with blood, and His name is the Word of God. The armies that were in heaven followed Him on white horses, wearing pure white linen. A sharp sword came from His mouth, so that He might strike the nations with it. He will shepherd them with an iron scepter. He will also trample the winepress of the fierce anger of God, the Almighty. And He has a name written on His robe and on His thigh:

Seven Signs Of The Second Coming Of Christ;

1. False Christ's. Matthew 24:5 For many will come in My name, saying, 'I am the Messiah,' and they will deceive many.

2. Wars and rumors of wars. Matthew 24:6 You are going to hear of wars and rumors of wars. See that you are not alarmed, because these things must take place, but the end is not yet.

3. Natural disasters. Matthew 24:7 For nation will rise up against nation, and kingdom against kingdom. There will be famines and earthquakes in various places.

4. Persecution of believers. Matthew 24:8-13 All these events are the beginning of birth pains. "Then they will hand you over for persecution, and they will kill you. You will be hated by all nations because of My name. Then many will take offense, betray one another and hate one another. Many false prophets will rise up and deceive many. Because lawlessness will multiply, the love of many will grow cold. But the one who endures to the end will be delivered.

5. Evangelization of the World. Matthew 24:14 This good news of the kingdom will be proclaimed in all the world as a testimony to all nations. And then the end will come.

6. Apostasy. Matthew 24:12 Because lawlessness will multiply, the love of many will grow cold.

7. Re-gathering of Israel. Isaiah 11:11 Many false prophets will rise up and deceive many.

BIBLE DOCTRINE

Timeline Of Eschatology

1. The Second Coming of Jesus Christ
    a. Christ comes to resurrect the dead saints and rapture the living saints. 1 Thessalonians 4:16-17 For the Lord Himself will descend from heaven with a shout, with the archangel's voice, and with the trumpet of God, and the dead in Christ will rise first. Then we who are still alive will be caught up together with them in the clouds to meet the Lord in the air and so we will always be with the Lord.
    b. They will be given glorified bodies and enjoy sweet fellowship with Christ at a grand marriage supper in heaven. Revelation 19:7-9 Let us be glad, rejoice, and give Him glory, because the marriage of the Lamb has come, and His wife has prepared herself. She was given fine linen to wear, bright and pure. For the fine linen represents the righteous acts of the saints.

2. Seven years of tribulation is when God will send plagues of judgments to punish the whole world. This is also called the seven bowls of judgments in Revelation 16.
    a. First 3yrs 6 mths will seam peaceful.
    b. Second 3yrs 6 months will chaotic with the manifestation of the anti-Christ.

c. The False Prophet and the Antichrist will perform miracles by Satan's power.

3. Battle of Armageddon.

    a. Battle in history will be launched against Israel at the Battle of Armageddon.

    b. Christ will return 2 Thessalonians 2:8 to save Israel as King of kings and Lord of lords, and defeat the enemies. Revelation 19:15-16 A sharp sword came from His mouth, so that He might strike the nations with it. He will shepherd them with an iron scepter. He will also trample the winepress of the fierce anger of God, the Almighty. And He has a name written on His robe and on His thigh:

4. The Antichrist and the False Prophet will be cast in the lake of fire. Revelation 19:20 But the beast was taken prisoner, and along with him the false prophet, who had performed the signs in his presence. He deceived those who accepted the mark of the beast and those who worshiped his image with these signs. Both of them were thrown alive into the lake of fire that burns with sulfur.

5. Millennium

    a. During the Millennium, Satan will be bound for a thousand years in the bottomless pit. Revelation 20:1-3 Then I saw an angel coming down from heaven with the key to the abyss and a great chain in his hand. He seized the dragon, that ancient serpent who is the Devil and Satan, and bound him for 1,000 years. He threw him into the abyss, closed it, and put a seal on it so that he would no longer deceive the nations until the 1,000 years were completed. After that, he must be released for a short time.

b. During the Millennium, Jesus will rule on earth with the raptured and resurrected saints from Jerusalem. Isaiah 2:1-4 The vision that Isaiah son of Amoz saw concerning Judah and Jerusalem: In the last days the mountain of the LORD'S house will be established at the top of the mountains and will be raised above the hills. All nations will stream to it, and many people will come and say, "Come, let us go up to the mountain of the LORD, to the house of the God of Jacob. He will teach us about His ways so that we may walk in His paths." For instruction will go out of Zion and the word of the LORD from Jerusalem. He will settle disputes among the nations and provide arbitration for many peoples. They will turn their swords into plows and their spears into pruning knives. Nations will not take up the sword against other nations, and they will never again train for war.

c. During the Millennium, there will be perfect peace, order, and harmony. Even in nature, lions will eat straw and children will play with snakes. Isaiah 65:25 The wolf and the lamb will feed together, and the lion will eat straw like the ox, but the serpent's food will be dust! They will not do what is evil or destroy on My entire holy mountain," says the LORD.

    d. During the Millennium, all Israel shall be saved and will worship Christ in a glorious temple. Romans 11:26 And in this way all Israel will be saved, as it is written: The Liberator will come from Zion; He will turn away godlessness from Jacob.

6. The Lake of Fire

    a. At the end of the thousand years, Satan will be released to stir up one final rebellion against God, and will be defeated and cast into the Lake of Fire and brimstone to burn forever. Revelation 20:13 Then the sea gave up its dead, and Death and Hades gave up their dead; all were judged according to their works.

    b. All the unsaved dead shall be resurrected, judged and cast into the lake of fire. Revelation 20:15 And anyone not found written in the book of life was thrown into the lake of fire.

7. Total Destruction to first heavens and the old Earth, which will be destroyed with fervent heat. 2 Peter 3:10 But the Day of the Lord will come like a thief; on that day the heavens will pass away with a loud

noise, the elements will burn and be dissolved, and the earth and the works on it will be disclosed.

8. New Heaven and a New Earth will appear together where God's people will dwell forever with the Lord. Revelation 21:1,2 Then I saw a new heaven and a new earth, for the first heaven and the first earth had passed away, and the sea no longer existed. I also saw the Holy City, new Jerusalem, coming down out of heaven from God, prepared like a bride adorned for her husband.

BIBLE DOCTRINE

BIBLIOGRAPHY

Apostles then and now – Mark Pfeifer.

Concise Theology series – Alan S. Bandy

Easton's Bible Dictionary

Jameson, Fausset, and Brown Commentary

Matthew Henry's Concise Commentary on the Whole Bible

New Illustrated Bible Dictionary – Ronald F. Youngblood

STRONGS Exhaustive Concordance – Hendrickson

Survey of the Old Testament – Paul N. Brown

Survey of the New Testament – Paul N. Brown

Systematic Theology – Wayne Grudem

The Early Days of Christianity – F.W. Farrar

The knowledge of the Holy – A.W.Tozer

Vitamins for your soul – Ps. Charles Gordon.

Willimingtons Guide to the Bible – Dr. H.L. Willmington

Scripture quotations taken from:

The Complete Jewish Study Bible.

King James Version, and the New King James Version.

Holmans Christian Standard Bible.

New American Standard Version and English Standard Version

New Living Translation and Amplified Bible.

FOUNDATIONS OF FAITH

More from Mark Visser

Get a copy for yourself and for a friend, through Amazon or Kindle

CONTACT DIRECT – mark_visser@me.com

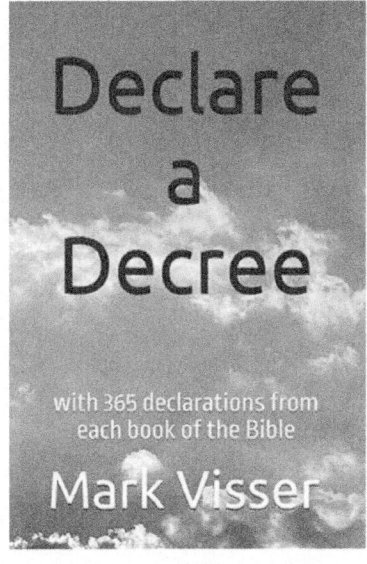

BIBLE DOCTRINE

Follow on Instagram: markvisser_prophet

Follow on YouTube: https://www.youtube.com/c/MarkVisserMinistries

Follow on Facebook: https://www.facebook.com/isaiah58markvisser

https://www.facebook.com/profile.php?id=100090692543289

Check out our Church Website: https://isaiah58church.org

Our is vision is Acts 1;8

We are empowered by The Holy Spirit to equip saints for ministry and win souls for the Kingdom of God.

We training and equipping in the prophetic, through teaching, imparting and delivering the now word of God and establishing prophetic wells.

Your seed into will help us continue building Prophetic Wells.

Prophetic Wells

Printed in Great Britain
by Amazon